THE FINE ART OF
Ice Skating

THE FINE ART OF

Ice
Skating

AN ILLUSTRATED
HISTORY AND
PORTFOLIO OF
STARS

JULIA WHEDON

HARRY N. ABRAMS, INC., PUBLISHERS,
NEW YORK

Excerpts from "Musée des Beaux Arts" by W. H. Auden. Copyright
1940 and renewed 1968 by W. H. Auden. Reprinted from *W. H.
Auden: Collected Poems*, edited by Edward Mendelson, by permission
of Random House, Inc.
Excerpts from *Competitive Figure Skating* by Robert S. Ogilvie,
Copyright 1985 by Robert S. Ogilvie and Joan A. Ogilvie. Reprinted
by permission of Harper & Row, Publishers, Inc.
Excerpt from "Winter Landscape," *Short Poems*, by John Berryman.
Copyright 1948, 1967 by John Berryman. Reprinted by permission
of Farrar, Straus and Giroux, Inc.
Excerpts from *The Skater's Handbook* by John Misha Petkevich.
Copyright © 1984 John Misha Petkevich. Reprinted with
the permission of Charles Scribner's Sons, an imprint of
Macmillan Publishing Co.

Editor: Lois Brown
Designers: Judith Michael and Gilda Hannah
Photo Editor: John Crowley

Text Copyright © 1988 by Julia Whedon
Published in 1988 by Harry N. Abrams, Incorporated, New York

Library of Congress Cataloging-in-Publication Data
Whedon, Julia.
    The fine art of ice skating: an illustrated history and portfolio
of stars/Julia Whedon.
        p. cm.
    Bibliography: p. 124
    ISBN 0-8109-1127-2
    1. Skating—History.   2. Skaters—Pictorial works.   I. Title.
GV850.4.W44   1988
796.91'09—dc19   88-5884

To the memory of my mother, Carroll Angell,
and to my daughters, Erika and Jessica.

"I live while I skate; I feel every motion; all the muscles speak and answer me, as it were. I talk with my arms, my shoulders, with all my limbs, and think of music — of flying, if you will."

George Meagher (1895)

CONTENTS

PREFACE

I didn't mean to write a history, and I don't think I have. An historian would have provided more detail and documentation, I'm sure. Indeed, any decent skating buff can quote you everything about everybody for the last hundred years. I was interested, instead, in the story of skating, which seemed to me to be full of vivid people, places, and incidents. I believed the general reader—a creature like myself—would welcome these stories and pictures, linked as they are, like delightful coincidences with so much we already know about the world. Beyond that, I hoped to interest skaters in their own history—something more dimensional than winning and performing. It was the great British skater, John Curry, who told me skaters had no book of their own. Certainly, the more skating is practiced by some as an art form, the greater the need for public appreciation of skating's origins and traditions, if it is ever to achieve the "legitimacy" dance enjoys.

Finally, I decided it was time for a simple explanation of what it is skaters do: How they get from the local rink to some Olympic skating complex, breathing hard and smiling. As the story of skating moves into the present tense, the reader will surmise that modern history is written largely in the careers of individual skaters. Skaters who change skating—adding to it, altering it—make history.

In preparing this essay, I have conducted my research both by computer, at the Library of Congress, and on my hands and knees in New England attics. Both experiences proved rewarding, as did many in between. I'd like to acknowledge some of these.

My thanks to the United States Figure Skating Association in Colorado Springs, especially to Pat Cataldi, for liberal access to both their photo archive and the elegant Gillis Grafstrom Collection; to Harvard's Widener Library and its retrieving undergraduates—an excellent sports collection is well represented in the appended bibliography; to the New York Society Library; Boston Atheneum; and Schlesinger Library at Radcliffe; to the New York and Boston public libraries; to the unflappable Sarah Bluestone at the Bettmann Archive; to Margaret Williamson, for her patience and interest; to Mrs. Carin Dohlman, Mrs. William Schwann, and Professor Norman Pettit, my thanks for their translations of Swedish, Finnish, and German documents; to Kestin Martinazzoli of Kokkola, Finland, for a candid correspondence about Jackson Haines; to Minnie Tucker Biggs, for her memories and mementos of Grandfather Irving Brokaw; to the patient Suzanne Gluck, my agent; and to Nina Payne and David Eames for honest comment and encouragement.

They all did their best to help. Any shortcomings are my own.

INTRODUCTION

ertain experiences change you and you never change back. The tangle of ropes and wire at a circus can change you. A black Steinway waiting on a concert stage can change you. The refrigerated smell of indoor skating ice changed me. I was about eight years old at the time. A friend took me to the Sonja Henie Rink in Westwood; I think it was Westwood, California. I remember it was winter because we couldn't go swimming. I'd never seen snow. Ice, I figured, was just one of those excellent technological things. I liked hunks of it in soft drinks; a whole room full of it seemed like a fine idea.

I remember it was cold and damp and dark inside the rink and that people were in a great hurry to rent skates and get them on their feet. I remember no one was allowed on the ice at first; life was full of rules like that. So it lay out there all waxy and smooth and valuable. Extravagant organ music began to fill the air. I struggled with my laces. Everyone was getting ahead of me, mincing around on the teeth of their blades, wearing wonderful velvet skirts and cabled sweaters; I hated them all. Then a gate opened and I saw the first blade cutting into the ice. . . . I see it still, shining, trailing a watery path. I hear the gouging sound of a jump, the silent landing. I see awkward people making their way round and round the rink traffic, the impudent speed of some kids stroking through the crowd, the honing sound of their hockey blades drawing a rueful glance from some decorous old lady. Older children, afraid of disgrace, hold onto the side rail; younger ones run full tilt between falls. And, in the center, horrid little girls in costumes made by their mothers fall out of jumps and spins in weary repetition, scornfully avoiding the rest of us who also need ice to skate. Time for a little hot chocolate, to rest these aching stricken feet. No, wait: I see a skater generating speed, easily threading through the lurching assembly, going somewhere, getting somewhere, being there, doing it, really doing it, coiling, lifting, soaring, landing—only to glide again until chance, time, and space afford another try.

That afternoon ended forty years ago holding hands with a G.I. He invited me to skate with him during the "twos." He must have seen me during the "all skate." He complimented me on my progress. He, of course, was perfect. We skated very fast and I didn't fall down, but I was in love and scared my parents would be mad. At last the session ended. We'd "cracked the whip" together, skating like crazy to catch the outstretched hand, his, then mine, then somebody else's, until all the willing skaters were jointed in a single wheeling, whipping line. The music stopped. We parted. I put on my shoes—numb with cold, joy, excitement, accomplishment, and the unbridled lust of those few afternoon hours. I tell this story to state my qualifications (I have omitted nothing about any later titles or medals) and to illustrate, as I hope to do, that nearly every important element in the evolution of skating history is present each time we skate. The ice beneath our feet, the rink, the blades, the crowds, romance, speed, spins, tricks, falls, games, music, costumes, contests, dancing, daring, and beauty are a syllabus to the working out, over a thousand years, of the possibilities of upright movement over a fast mischievous surface.

SKATING THROUGH A THOUSAND WINTERS

hink about ice. . . . In the fall of 1983 thirty-five Russian ships lay trapped in the ice-choked zone between the East Siberian and Chukchi Seas. An epic struggle to free them had been going on for nearly a month. Hulls punctured, cracked, crumpled, sank. A sixteen-thousand-ton nuclear-powered ice breaker lost a two-ton propeller blade in one lunge against the pack—then twenty miles wide and six feet thick. "We've gathered massive technical means into one mighty fist," a Soviet administrator announced. "We'll pound this cursed ice until we saw the entire Chukchi Sea in half." With this, they resumed their heroic efforts. Engines screaming, hulls shuddering, they rammed and mounted the ice, again and again, crushing it beneath their own great weight, only to watch it form anew, cementing the floating floes behind them. . . .

Consider the Columbia glacier in Alaska, a river of ice forty miles long. It expels thirty million tons of ice into the waters at Valdez. Every day. Some portions are two hundred and fifty feet high and two miles wide. Higher than Niagara Falls and wider by far. The glacier booms and thunders as it moves forward, twenty feet a day, an inch every six minutes. In describing glaciers, experts speak of their heads, their eyes, their tongues, their dorsal and ventral sides. They calve. They heal. Clearly, they are alive in our language—and in our imaginations as well. Imagine that they covered most of the European and North American continents for the last million years. "Chicago, London, and New York," one writer observed, "were once part of an enormous skating pond with the United States and the Soviet Union stuck together at the Bering Sea." But that was then; we've been thawing for the last seventeen thousand years. We're in the Fourth Postglacial Period. The next ice age is approaching, however: Slowly. Crack. Boom.

Think of the power of ice on the move, gouging out mountain passes, diverting rivers, soaking up oceans, filling in lakes. It is surpassed only by its fragility and elegance. Look closely at its architecture. Magnify the crystals. See prisms, needles, flowers, branching stars. What a paradox. Such gaiety and lightness, such variety. Now look again. There's no variety at all. Other crystals assume thirty-two different geometric forms; ice is always hexagonal. Always. And it always forms at 0° Centigrade in fresh water, 2° Centigrade in sea water. And, at these temperatures, it dependably expands, becoming less dense than water, and floats. Ice will also, predictably, reject four-fifths of any salt present in its original form. You can count on ice. If you're not an ocean liner. . . .

Remember the night of April 15, 1912, somewhere south of Newfoundland and east of New York. The

———————

S.S. Titanic was crossing the North Atlantic on her maiden voyage. She was a celebrity. She was beautiful, sophisticated, indomitable. Then she touched an iceberg and sank like a stone, taking fifteen hundred passengers with her. Like the incineration of the *Hindenburg*, the incident greatly diminished man's sense of his own power. For a while.

*   *   *

Sometimes, looking at the pictures of winters past—so abundant, silent, and profound—we feel a stab of regret, something lost: that transformation once so frightening, so exhilarating, so important. Emerson knew those winters:

> *Announced by all the trumpets of the sky,*
> *Arrives the snow, and driving o'er the fields,*
> *Seems nowhere to alight: the whited air*
> *Hides hills and woods, the river, and the heaven,*
> *And veils the farm-house at the garden's end.*
> *The sled and traveler stopped, the courier's feet,*
> *Delayed, all friends shut out, the housemates set*
> *Around the radiant fireplace, enclosed*
> *In a tumultuous privacy of storm.*

Remember, imagine, stepping into such a landscape—a world stunned, wildly beautiful, there at your door. "The mad wind's night work," Emerson called it, "the frolic architecture of the snow." Sliding, sledding, sleighing, skiing, skating—all express the rapture, music felt within, when winter comes again.

Why is it the winters in poetry, art, and memory seem deeper—more extreme? Were winters once colder or are we just older?

The *Encyclopedia Perthenis* tells us that Great Frosts struck with frequency and regularity from 200 A.D. well into the late 1800s.

From the 1891 Paris edition of the *Herald Tribune:*

Below: Skating *à deux* in the French Alps. (World F.S. Hall of Fame and Museum)

Opposite top: A small band of enthusiasts tests the shore ice—a freak of Alaska weather—at Valdez, 1905. (Library of Congress)

Opposite bottom: "The best skaters have always come from the big cities, where they would draw a crowd—then be ordered off the ice."—Irving Brokaw, *The Art of Skating*. In front of the Dakota Apartments, Central Park, New York City, c. 1900. (Library of Congress)

A good freeze celebrated at Davos, Switzerland, international skating headquarters by the 1870s. (World F.S. Hall of Fame and Museum)

There is still no sign of a breaking up of the severe frost which has prevailed almost without intervention for nine weeks. Skating is going on upon the widest parts of the Thames at Kingston, where the ice is now 12 to 15 inches thick. Arrangements have been made to hold a carnival on the river opposite Hampton Church tomorrow. An actual printing press is to be set up on the ice and a sheep will be roasted.

A quarter century earlier the *London Graphic* caviled, "When the Thames freezes the ice is almost as unfit for skating as a street with the pavement up."

This earlier report from another London resident:

When the Great Fenne or Moore (which washeth the walles of the citie on the north side) is frozen, many young men play upon the yce. . . . Some tye bones to their feete, and under their heeles, and shoving themselves by a little picked staffe, doe slide as swiftlie as a birde flyeth in the aire, or an arrow out of a crosse-bow. Sometimes two runne together with poles, and hitting one the other, either one or both doe fall, not without hurt; some break their armes, some their legs, but youth desirous of glorie, in this sort exerciseth it selfe against the time of warre.

The chronicler is William FitzStephen, clerk to Thomas à Becket, writing in the cold of 1190 A.D., fully seven hundred years before the others. The passage not only captures the daring, calamity, and beauty of skating but stands as the first written account of skating in England and, as such, may be considered an announcement of the beginnings of skating as sport.

Skating was not indigenous to England because it was not necessary to England. We know it was imported either by the Saxons in 1056 or the Normans in 1066. Skating for the fun of it is the skating we enjoy today. It is related to, but distinct from, the more ancient and generic practice of "sliding" common to many frigid climes.

* * *

A blizzard of winters separates us from the origins of "skating-sliding." We can barely make them out. There is a pair of skates at the *Stadbibliotek* in Berne, Switzerland, said to be four thousand years old. They are made of bone. They have a waxy sheen. Blunt and useful, they look like the implements of early man. They are. Tools for dealing with a frozen world. You need only "tye them to your feete and under the heeles, shove along with a picked staffe, to flye like an arrow out of a crosse-bow." This was the skating FitzStephen saw. While a recent import to England, it had been going on in about the same manner for eons, but hardly as a sport.

Sliding is the shared spontaneous invention of all people besieged by frozen water and terrain—in Scandinavia, the Netherlands, parts of Asia, North America, the Arctic. It is simply the human thing to do. Children reinvent it every time they see a frozen puddle.

The distinction between sliding and skating exists most vividly in the pedant's mind perhaps. The Norseman cared not. Slip, slide, ski, skate, what did it matter as long as you got there? But the etymologist gets upset when language is indistinct, untidy in its messages. The word "skate" comes from a family of words that translates as "clog" or "stilt"—a device put on the feet to raise one off the ground. Confusion arises from the fact that the well-dressed Norseman had a number of these and we can't always tell from his stories which he was wearing for what. His skis had flat runners of course, but then so did his skates—both of them—his ice skates and his snow skates. He had clogs as well, fitted with spikes, for managing on the ice. All this he called skating.

The Sagas, "that wonderful Scandinavian literature whose poetical myths, stirring narratives, and thrilling romances treated of all the most interesting phases of human life, at a time when literature of the rest of Europe was almost wholly confined to the dog-latin of the monks," wrote Neville Goodman, a nineteenth-century skating historian, "is full of allusions to this art." The *Elder Edda*, a collection of Icelandic literature gathered by Saemund the Wise at the turn of the eleventh century, tales dating back to 156 A.D., remarks on the God Uller's "beauty, arrows and skates."

But were those really skates?

Best not ask. Press on to what is known. That in time the design was altered, improved, and with it skating technique. Bone skates were succeeded by blunt iron skates with iron runners, then steel—such as we use today. These last two had, have, the skater running on the narrow edge, not the flat, as if the flat had been turned on its side, which it had, either by accident or design. This radical change came in the seventeenth century. But stop. We must circle back to an earlier change before we pass it by.

* * *

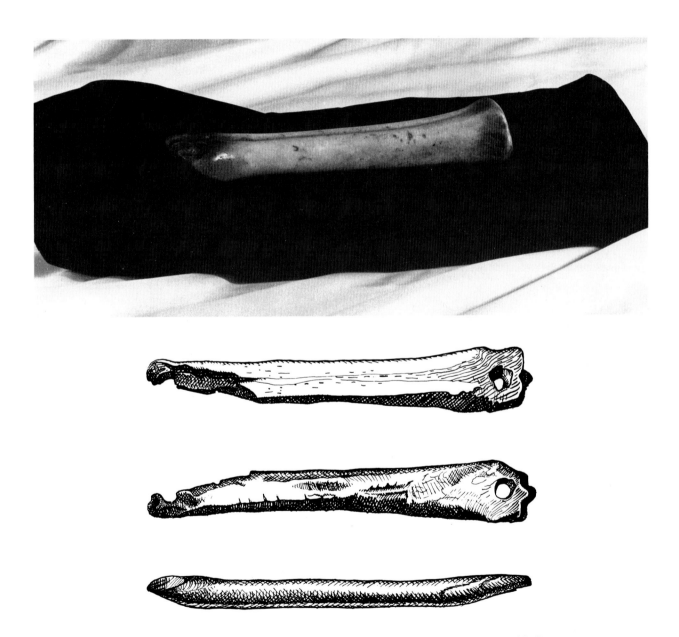

Thousand-year-old sporting goods: bone skates, ancient tools for coping with a once frozen world. Bone runners were strapped with leather thongs to the feet. (World F.S. Hall of Fame and Museum)

Saint Lydwina, after her historic fall in 1396. Wood engraving by Johannes Brugman, 1498. (World F.S. Hall of Fame and Museum)

Just as there are historic first words connected with skating, there is a first picture. It is a woodcut executed in 1498 by Johannes Brugman in Schiedam, Holland. It depicts an event that transpired in 1396, two hundred years after the FitzStephen account. Its subject is Lydwina, patron saint of ice skating—and, and in a sense, of falling down, a subject never far from one's thoughts when there's talk of skating.

Lydwina, the story goes, was born in Schiedam in 1380 of "poor, but ancient and honorable parents," according to the account of Thomas à Kempis, the German ecclesiastic (and her exact contemporary). She was ailing as a child, but in time grew into a robust and beautiful young woman. In 1396, when she was sixteen, she was visited by friends just prior to the feast of Candlemas. They invited her to go skating on the frozen *Shei*. Lydwina declined; she wasn't feeling well. The others insisted. She relented, being an agreeable sort. But to her sorrow. She was "knocked down on rough ice by one of her girl companions, and broke a rib." Thereafter, she fell victim to a succession of "frightful diseases" that she bore with astonishing fortitude for the next thirty-eight years, until her death in 1413. For her suffering and forbearance she was beatified in 1616, and sanctified in 1890. A number of miracles have since been attributed to the power of her spirituality—chief among them, the uncanny protection of Schiedam through the bombings of World War II.

This picture has more to tell: first, that skating was considered a suitable enterprise for both men and women, and second, that iron skates had arrived. This is not so much announced as it is implied by the figure of the man approaching the fallen Lydwina, slightly right of center. He's not shuffling and sliding forward but advancing by leaning and rolling—a technique made possible by the bite of iron on the ice. The leg kicked out to one side is the giveaway.

A general word here about falling. Mocked, feared, tolerated, it is always with us—in fact, and in art. Few artists who interested themselves in skating scenes failed to miss the humor and peril of the human condition at $-2°$ Centigrade. Falling plagues the best and the rest of us. This from John Curry, 1976 British Olympic gold medalist:

I fell, badly, on the average of thirty or forty times a day. My embarrassment knew no bounds. There I was, supposedly one of the best skaters in the world, and all that anybody saw of me was an endless series of slides across the ice . . . in a crumpled heap against the barrier.

The Skaters, a gouache drawing by Francisco Goya, 1819. (Museum of Fine Arts, Boston)

And from Lord Templewood, author of *Modern Figure Skating:*

The most helpless moment of my life . . . I do not mean when I was born, for that is the most desperate hour in the life of a man, but rather when I first set skate to ice. That is when your friends say to you, "do not push off with your toe, bend your knees," and all you are thinking about is why you ever got on the ice and how you will ever get off it. You cannot start and you cannot stop. You cannot move and you cannot stand still.

"Go down like a rope, not a stack of wood, a piece at a time," Sonja Henie advised. "You can even get to like it."

Given the obvious risks, what makes people skate? Ernest Jones, the eminent biographer of Freud wrote: "It combines and surpasses the joys of flying and dancing; only in a certain type of dream do we ever else attain a higher degree of the same ravishing experience of exultantly skimming the earth." Eric Nesterenko, the eminent Chicago Black Hawk, concurred. "Some nights you just go. You can't stop. The rhythm gets to you, or the speed. You're moving, man, moving and that's all."

4

HG. Inuet. J.S. sculp.

Accumulant homines totum quęcynɡ per annum,
Hęc ego confumo, foli hęc mihi cuncta parautur.

C.S.

THE DUTCH: A WHOLE SOCIETY ON ICE

*F*or a thousand years skating history was written upon ponds, lakes, rivers, inland seas, and canals. Terrain was everything. And for a time skating was central to one of the most powerful nations in the world—the Netherlands. Canals were the veins and arteries of a corpus grown fat and rich on trade in fish, wool, tin, woven cloth, cattle, and, finally, art. Bruges was once richer and more powerful than Paris. The palace at Brussels was home to the Holy Roman Emperor, nominal ruler of more than half of Europe. Antwerp was the richest trading city in all the world. When the canals froze, something had to be done. Skates were to the Dutch what gondolas were to the Venetians: an absolute necessity turned national treasure.

The fine points of canal skating are explained by Pieter Brueghel in *Gate at Antwerp* (1553). It involved slipping, sliding, talking, falling, dawdling, gawking, scoffing, pushing, pointing, peeking, giggling, chasing, drowning, freezing, hugging, and yelling. In short, life itself. A whole society moved out on the ice, and Brueghel saw it. Folkways, foibles, customs, commerce—and art—moved outside, away from somber themes and interiors. This humanizing of thought and art must have come as a great relief. W. H. Auden, seeing what they saw, said it best:

> *About suffering they were never wrong,*
> *The Old Masters: how well they understood*
> *Its human position; how it takes place*
> *While someone else is eating or opening a window or just walking dully along;*
> *How, when the aged are reverently, passionately waiting*
> *For the miraculous birth, there always must be*
> *Children who did not specially want it to happen, skating*
> *On a pond at the edge of the wood. . . .*

The precise value of the oblivious children in those lines is sounded by Brueghel in *The Hunters in the Snow* (1565). The weariness of the hunters in the foreground, their heaviness, is the more deeply felt for the lightness of the distant skaters. One of a seasonal series painted in the same year by Brueghel, it is among the first great paintings about weather. For many of us, it's what we mean by winter. The lingering

"They pretend that winter is not a season of cold and death." Engraving by Jan van de Velde, c. 1593–1641. (World F.S. Hall of Fame and Museum)

———

impact of those hunters and their dogs, the trees, the skaters, was the clear inspiration in these lines of John Berryman:

> The three men coming down the winter hill
> In brown, with tall poles and a pack of hounds,
> At heel, through the arrangement of the trees,
> Past the five figures at the burning straw,
> Returning cold and silent to their town,
>
> Returning to the drifted snow, the rink
> lively with children, to the older men
> The long companions they can never reach,
> The blue light, men with ladders, by the church,
> The sledges and shadow in the twilit street,
>
> Are not aware that in the sandy time
> To come, the evil waste of history
> Outstretched, they will be seen upon the brow
> Of that same hill: when all their company
> Will have been irrecoverably lost . . . .

That rink "lively with children" is also the first such, so far as we know, ever to have been painted. Upon close inspection (the natural reaction to a Brueghel painting), we see curling, hockey, and plain skating, all ongoing in a contrived skating space. A small thing—but not to skaters; such contrivances would eventually bring skating to the whole world, from the peaks of the Himalayas to the deserts of Saudi Arabia.

Apart from the delight and commercial profit that came of canal skating, the canals—with their limitless connected skating passages—produced skaters of exceptional speed and endurance. Racing and touring were drawn out of the Dutch by their terrain just as figure skating was later extruded from the English town-skater confined, as he was, to doodle on ponds, lakes, and the occasional river.

Toward the end of the sixteenth century, the great power of the Netherlands was to be tested by the

Opposite top: The gentrification of Dutch canal skating. "Hyems," Matthijss Bril the Younger, c. 1550–1584. (World F.S. Hall of Fame and Museum)

Opposite bottom: The fine points of canal skating illustrated by Pieter Brueghel in *Gate at Antwerp*, 1553. Engraving by Ioan Galle. (World F.S. Hall of Fame and Museum)

Below: By the seventeenth century, the Dutch were moving with great skill across the ice. Rembrandt shows us a competent skater in this copper engraving, c. 1639. (The Pierpont Morgan Library, New York. B.156)

———————

Spanish. United in their desire not to be united by an absent Spanish king, the provinces fought for their independence against the armies of King Philip. All but beaten in the winter of 1572, the Dutch fleet found itself locked in the frozen waters at Amsterdam. Adding insult to injury, they were then attacked by a detachment of Spanish soldiers fitted out with spiked clogs. The Dutch rallied and routed the Spanish on skates. The Duke of Alva, it is said, was so impressed with the victory that he promptly ordered seven thousand pairs of skates for his own men. He later abandoned the idea when, after a year, his troops still couldn't skate in formation.

In the years that followed, the Dutch secured their independence but lost the great sway of their commercial and political power. Yet, through it all, skating thrived and prevailed. Indeed, skating became a popular export.

Tilting, as illustrated by Stanley Berkeley in the *Chatterbox*. (Mary Evans Picture Library)

THEIR MAJESTIES: THE ROYALS ON ICE

*S*kating was introduced not once but three times before becoming firmly established in England. After the bone skating FitzStephen saw in the winter of 1190, not another mention was made of it for the next five hundred years. We know that in that time war, famine, fire, and disease swept England; weather, too, may have been a consideration. Whatever the explanation, what we do know is that recorded skating history resumes on a specific date: December 1, 1662. Two diarists, both Londoners, one a later Lord of the Admiralty, the other later Secretary of the Royal Society, saw people skating and thought the sight sufficiently remarkable to note. A sampling from the first Samuel Pepys gives us a sense of that important winter:

November 27, 1662: At my waking, I found the tops of houses covered with snow, which is a very rare sight, that I have not seen these three years . . .

November 30, 1662: It is a bitter cold frost today . . .

December 1, 1662: Thence I to my Lord Sandwich's . . . to talk a little about business; and then over to the Parke (where I first in my life, it being a great frost, did see people sliding with their skeats, which is a very pretty art) . . . to St. James', where we all met to a venison pasty, and were very merry.

December 5, 1662: Up, it being a snow and hard frost . . .

December 7, 1662: A great snow, and so to church this morning.

December 11, 1662: Up, it being a great frost upon the snow . . .

December 12: From a very hard frost, when I awoke, I find a very great thaw, and my house overflown with it, which vexed me.

December 15, 1662: Up and to my Lord's and thence to the Duke and followed him into the Park, where, though ice was broken and dangerous, yet he would go slide upon his scates, which I did not like but he slides very well.

And from the other diarist, John Evelyn:

December 1, 1662: Having seen the strange and marvelous dexterity of the sliders in the new canal in St. James Parke performing before their Maties by divers gentlemen and others with their scheets after the manner of Hollanders, with what swiftness they passe, how suddenly they stop in full carriere upon the ice . . . .

That the silence should have been broken by two of the most singular social historians of that or any period makes it a proud moment indeed. But there's more to know. The "Maties" were majesties—most important, Charles II. The Duke seen "sliding very well" by an apprehensive Pepys was the Duke of York, brother of Charles II, who later acceded to the throne as James II.

Skating was back and back in style: it had become the royal thing to do. Aristocrats must have been stumbling all over themselves to learn this "pretty art," seeing how well it pleased the King. And well it might; he'd imported it himself from Holland. Born there, he later returned to Holland during his father's exile. Looking for action, it seems, he and his young courtiers found it skating on the frozen canals. The hard frost of 1662 apparently offered the first opportunity for that royal display of skating talent reported by Pepys and Evelyn. It is generally agreed that if such had existed beforehand Pepys, for one, certainly would have noticed and told us.

In actual point of fact, skating had already been smuggled into the nether regions during Cromwell's reign. The great Protestant reformer had ordered the draining of the fens, fourteen hundred square miles of bog, located on the eastern coast of Britain. Logically, a Dutch engineer and an army of Dutch prisoners were set to work building a canal system. Then, seeing the canals freeze over, the Dutch passed along another skill as well: Fen skating, the English equivalent of canal skating. It came to full flower in the nineteenth century in the person of William "Turkey" Smart of Welney, and his brother "Fish" (George), each of whom defended the championship title for ten years—only to lose it to an interloper, brother James. "If skating be the poetry of motion, speed-skating or fen skating, as it is sometimes called, is the epic as distinguished from the lyric branch of the art."

Hard freezes and good skating continued throughout the seventeenth century, much as Pepys described. The Thames flooded and froze (there being no embankment at the time, indeed, not until the nineteenth century) serving up acre upon acre of good skating at Chelsea and above the marsh between Lambeth and Kensington, according to the historian Christopher Hibbert. "In the winter of 1683–1684 there was so hard a frost that not only streets of booths were put upon the frozen Thames and oxen roasted on the ice, but horses and carts and carriages were driven over it from bank to bank."

The Frost Fair continued throughout the month of January with more and more booths and tents, cock-shops, barbers-shops and donkey sheds erected beneath the bridge. Teams of apprentices played football

Parisians skating, *pour le sport*. Both Marie Antoinette and Napoleon indulged, she in the Bois, he on the moat at Auxerre—where he nearly drowned. Lithograph by Vernet, from *Le Bon Genre de Paris*, 1810. (The Bettmann Archive)

Skaters on the Serpentine in Hyde Park by Julius Caesar Ibbetson. A watercolor dated 1786. (National Gallery of Art)

FROST FAIR ON THE RIVER THAMES, 1884.

Monday February the 4: 1684

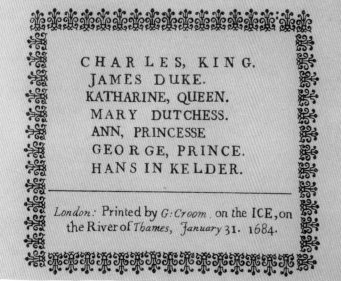

CHARLES, KING.
JAMES DUKE.
KATHARINE, QUEEN.
MARY DUTCHESS.
ANN, PRINCESSE
GEORGE, PRINCE.
HANS IN KELDER.

London: Printed by G: Croom, on the ICE, on the River of Thames, January 31. 1684.

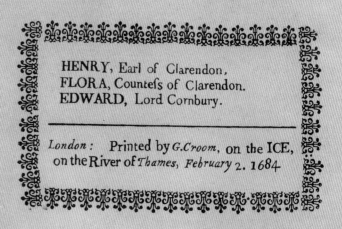

HENRY, Earl of Clarendon.
FLORA, Countefs of Clarendon.
EDWARD, Lord Cornbury.

London: Printed by G.Croom, on the ICE, on the River of Thames, February 2. 1684

All of London moved out on the ice for the sheer joy of it. Frost Fair on the River Thames, 1684. (Mary Evans Picture Library)

and hockey while their girlfriends cheered them on, eating mince pies and keeping their hands warm with baked potatoes. A printer put up a press and for sixpence sold a bordered card with the buyer's name and date inscribed in it together with the inscription: printed on the river Thames it being frozen over. In the 36th year of King Charles II.

Interrupted by a sudden thaw, one of the last of these great frost fairs was seen majestically floating out to sea on the tide.

Not to be outdone by the English, the French took up skating as well. They saw at once the possibilities for style and elegance and exploited them fully. Skating once again found royal favor—this time in the court of Louis XVI; Marie Antoinette, it is said, waited eagerly for the waters to freeze in the *Bois de Boulogne*.

And as Comte D'Avaux, French ambassador to the Netherlands, observed:

Twas a very extraordinary thing to see the Princess of Orange, with very short petticoats, and those tucked half way to her waist, and with iron pattins on her feet, learning to slide, sometimes on one foot, sometimes on the other, to oblige her husband the Duke of Monmouth.

The Chevalier de Saint George—a great fencer—was reputed to be a fine skater as well. Curious, the interest of both the Duke and the Chevalier. The Duke was the illegitimate son of Charles II whose sporting ways were reported by John Evelyn. The Chevalier was the youngest son of James II about whom we learned from Samuel Pepys. Second generation skating, evidence it was firmly rooted in England.

Skating had reached across Europe to Russia as well. Or rather, Russia—in the person of Peter the Great—had reached out to the West for everything Western. Like Marco Polo, he'd traveled abroad and come home with astonishing new ideas about everything. Mingling with the common people, doing as they did, he acquired the practical skills and information that were to bring his own country into the modern era. Needless to say, during a visit to Holland he learned skating from the Dutch. He is alleged, moreover, to have devised the first boot-mounted skate—a hundred years ahead of its official Western "invention."

THE ART AND SCIENCE OF SKATING

*I*nterest in skating became ever more serious. By mid-eighteenth century, it became practically a science. The English experimented endlessly with Dutch skate design; blades, by this time, were mounted on the edge, not the flat. Long runners with whimsical prows like treble clefs were all very well for speeding headlong down a canal but something different was called for when it came to refined skating, English skating. The Dutch were toying with simple big curving figures ("in a shame-faced sort of way," as one observer put it). But the English wanted to develop backward skating. They curved the blade slightly, added a groove, then extended it past the heel. And with that, the first figure skate was produced. The year was 1750.

The creation of the figure skate liberated and revolutionized skating causing a great rush to organize and set standards. While it's easy enough to judge who's faster, how do you decide who's better? The best English skaters clubbed together to set rules and standards. Those same rules and regulations, amplified, now extend to fill a book of more than three hundred pages. But it all began with one test: a complete circle skated on one foot, a complete circle skated on the other foot, followed by the nimble jumping of one, two, then three hats set out upon the ice. The satisfactory commission of these tasks admitted you to the ranks of the first skating club, the Edinburgh, established in 1750.

From a poem honoring the Edinburgh S.C.:

> *This snell and frosty morning,*
> *With rhind and trees adorning,*
> *Tho' Phoebus below,*
> *Through the sparkling snow,*
> *A skating we go,*
> *With a fal, lal, lal, lal, lal, lal,*
> *To the sound of the merry horn.*
>
> *From the right to the left we are plying,*
> *Swifter than winds we're flying,*
> *Spheres and spheres surrounding,*
> *Health and strength abounding,*

Page 42: *The Skater* by Gilbert Stuart, 1782. William Grant laying down figures of eight on the frozen Serpentine in London. American skaters caused a sensation abroad. (National Gallery of Art)

Opposite top: "The Dutch toyed with figures in a shame-faced sort of way." Eighteenth-century skates. (New York Public Library)

Opposite bottom: The English extended the heel, added a groove, and produced the first figure skate. A curly prow skate, c. 1850. (World F.S. Hall of Fame and Museum)

————

> *In circles we sweep,*
> *Our poise still we keep,*
> *Behold how we sweep,*
> *The face of the deep,*
> *With a fal, lal, lal, lal, lal, lal*
> *To the merry sound of the horn.*

Which is more than enough of that.

Considering two circles and three hats put you in the company of the best skaters of the day, it's staggering to contemplate all that developed. This from a text written by champion Bror Meyer about one hundred and seventy years later:

The head must be held in line with the back, which is to be kept hollowed; the shoulder should be carried in a natural position, the arms must not be raised but must be kept under control, yet not stiffened. They should be held at the side of the body, with the wrist slightly bent, so that the hands do not appear lifeless. The fingers must not be clenched nor yet spread apart . . . the foot does not descend heavily upon the ice . . . the front part of the skate reaches the ice close to the heels of the other foot . . . the unemployed foot gives a slight push-off from the side of the skate.

One hundred and thirteen words of advice and no mention yet of the figure to be skated.

"Textbook" skating began, in fact, with Robert Jones' *Treatise On Skating* in 1772 and was soon followed by publications in Germany and France: *Ueber das Scrittshuhfahren*, 1790, and *Le Vrai Patineur*, 1813.

*   *   *

With the science and practice of skating well under way, the enterprise began to enjoy a certain conservative respectability. Sir Henry Raeburn, the fashionable portrait painter who counted among his subjects Scott, Hume, Boswell, and Lord Melville, also painted a Reverend Walker skating on Duddingston Loch. Dr. Walker clearly survived the experience without loss to his professional dignity or social standing.

44

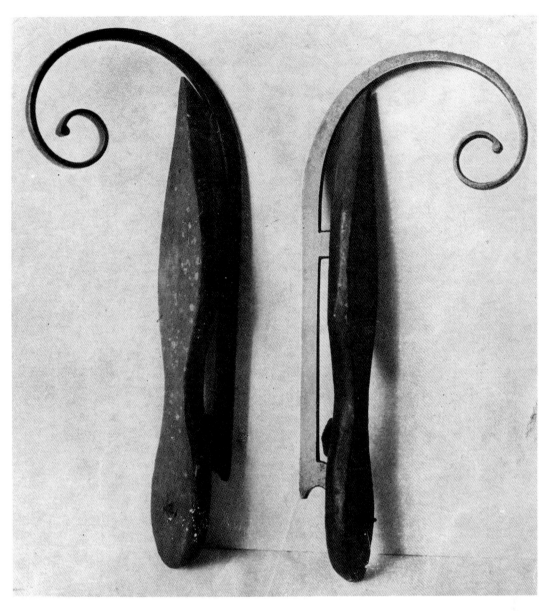

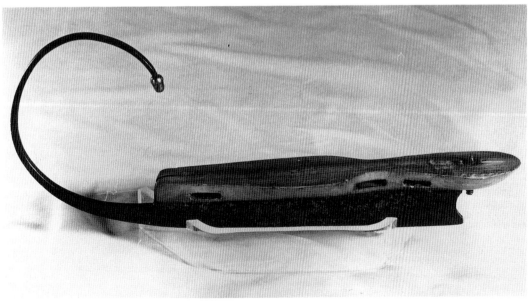

Illustration from the first French skating text, *Le Vrai Patineur*, by Jean Garcin, 1813. Demonstration of the *réverénce en ligne directe*—or spreadeagle, as the English prefer. (World F.S. Hall of Fame and Museum)

At about this same time, American painter Gilbert Stuart exhibited his masterpiece, *The Skater*. Stuart served as chief apprentice to the renowned American artist (and later President of the Royal Academy in London) Benjamin West—about whom, more in a moment. Stuart's credibility as an artist of the first rank was seriously compromised by the gossip that, while he could paint heads and create a "magical likeness," he couldn't draw or paint a body "below the fifth button." Stuart's answer to the charge was his portrait of William Grant, *The Skater*, seen gliding in St. James Park with the towers of Westminster Abbey rising in the distance. Grant appears to be skating "eights," which along with "threes" and "spreadeagles" were the first of the technical tricks to make up fancy skating. "If the chill luminous landscape . . . carries small conviction," one critic wrote, "the figure is splendid. Seldom were manliness and grace more winningly joined." Stuart's interest in skating, incidentally, was one he shared with his mentor, Benjamin West—an enthusiast of some considerable accomplishment.

From the annals of the Philadelphia Skating Club:

West once formed the acquaintance on Philadelphia ice of the Col. Howe—the General Howe of the Colonial War, but the resulting friendship dissolved with the spring thaw and was soon forgotten. One day, the painter having crossed the ocean, was skating on the Serpentine and amazing Londoners by the grace and rapidity of his motions. Some one suddenly exclaimed, "West!" "West!" It was Colonel Howe. "I am glad to see you," said he, "and not the less so that you can come in good time to vindicate my praises of American skating." He called to him Lord Spencer Hamilton, and some of the Cavendishes, to whom he introduced West as one of the Philadelphia prodigies, and requested him to show what was called "The Salute." West performed the feat so much to their satisfaction that they went away, spreading over London the praises of the American skater.

"Nor was the considerate Quaker," another source reported, "insensible to the value of such commendation. He continued to frequent the Serpentine and to gratify large crowds by cutting 'The Philadelphia Salute.'"

A man of protean accomplishments—writer-politician, clergyman-poet, West appears also to have been the first painter-skater-show-off. More than that, he is the first skater to have brought word from the Colonies of the exceptional state of the art being practiced there.

By the end of the eighteenth century, all the great poets and philosophers of nature had spoken. Their reverence for nature cannot be exaggerated. Coleridge, no athlete but an habitual walker, had logged an estimated one hundred eighty thousand miles by mid-life. John Constable, the artist, had actually attempted to collect and classify clouds; each of his studies carried a notation as to month, time of day, and wind direction. In Goethe, poet, novelist, dramatist, statesman, botanist, are met the powers of nature and romanticism to an almost unbelievable degree. A passionate skater, he reports in his memoirs, "It was while abandoning myself to the aimless movements that the most noble aspirations, which had too long lain dormant within me, were awaked; and I owe to these hours, which seemed lost, the most rapid and successful development of my potential projects."

The poet Wordsworth found inspiration not only while skating but in skating itself. He speaks of his skating at Hawkshead in the lake district of England where he was sent to school at an early age after the loss of both parents. From *The Prelude*, Book One:

> And in the frosty season, when the sun
> Was set, and visible for many a mile
> The cottage windows blazed through twilight gloom,
> I heeded not their summons: happy time
> It was indeed for all of us—for me
> It was a time of rapture! Clear and loud
> The village clock tolled six,—I wheeled about,
> Proud and exulting like an untired horse
> That cares not for his home. All shod with steel,
> We hissed along the polished ice in games
> Confederate, imitative of the chase
> And woodland pleasure,—the resounding horn,
> The pack loud chiming, and the hunted hare.
> So through the darkness and the cold we flew,
> And not a voice was idle; with the din
> Smitten, the precipices rang aloud;
> The leafless trees and every icy crag
> Tinkled like iron; while far distant hills

Into the tumult sent an alien sound
Of melancholy not unnoticed, while the stars
Eastward were sparkling clear, and in the west
The orange sky of evening died away.
Not seldom from the uproar I retired
Into a silent bay, or sportively
Glanced sideway, leaving the tumultous throng,
To cut across the reflex of a star
That fled, and, flying still before me, gleamed
Upon the glassy plain; and oftentimes,
When we had given our bodies to the wind,
And all the shadowy banks on either side
Came sweeping through the darkness, spinning still
The rapid line of motion, then at once
Have I, reclining back upon my heels,
Stopped short; yet still the solitary cliffs
Wheeled by me—even as if the earth had rolled
With visible motion her diurnal round!
Behind me did they stretch in solemn train,
Feebler and feebler, and I stood and watched
Till all was tranquil as a dreamless sleep.

＊   ＊   ＊

By the beginning of the nineteenth century, so great was the British enthusiasm for skating, they inexplicably collected and sent sixty tons of ice skates to South America. In the mighty freeze of 1814, they set up a printing press on the frozen Thames and published a book, *Frostiana*, exhorting people to skate and advising them on the fine points. "When practicing the outside edge," it read, "the right hand pocket

The Reverend Robert Walker Skating at Duddingston Loch by Sir Henry Raeburn, 1798. The very picture of bourgeois respectability. (National Gallery of Scotland)

Johann Wolfgang von Goethe, painter, poet, playwright, and passionate skater. Under mother's watchful eye, on the river Main at Frankfurt. William van Kaulback, 1805–1874. (World F.S. Hall of Fame and Museum)

of the skater's jacket should be weighted with shot and a bag of shot or weighty article should be carried in the right hand." "Dutch skates," it advised, "are not as finely shaped as those we have in England and the skaters are more remarkable for their ease than for their elegance." To compose and publish a critical essay while standing on a block of ice is a perfect demonstration of British *sang-froid*, for which they are justifiably famous.

The French, meanwhile, were not idle. With the publication of *Le Vrai Patineur* in 1813, came the first attempt at naming certain skating moves—a work that advocated a stylistic practice and generally was regarded as well ahead of its time. The British did not agree. The author "devoted himself largely, as might be expected, to steps, jumps, and poses, under highly fanciful names," remarked G. Herbert Fowler, a nineteenth-century authority in these matters. He gave as examples *reverence* (for "spreadeagle"), *pas de chasse* (for "on to Richmond forward"). Perhaps time will prove the best judge as to which terms were the more fanciful. In all probability Mr. Fowler's ill-concealed disdain may have been for the French school of skating itself, which differed markedly from the English. A group of French artists and intellectuals, known as the *Gilets Rouges* because of the red vests they affected, had taken up skating and expanded the British repertoire with new steps, pirouettes, and jumps. Great emphasis was placed, need we say, on style, grace, *attitude*. "Toesteps, spins, and pirouettes, can hardly be described as skating, in the English sense of the word," Fowler grumbled. The English skater ascribed, instead, to a kind of poker elegance. There was a correct, if not exact, way to do this thing. The rules of the London Skating Club, chartered in 1830, stated that no gentleman should be eligible for membership unless he could to skate the "Forward Cross Roll," "The Backward Cross Roll" and a large "Three" on each foot to the satisfaction of the Committee. "Ladies," it continued without apology, "shall skate freely forward in such a manner as to satisfy any two members of the Committee."

One couldn't be too rigorous or watchful. Not a year later, *Blackwood's Edinburgh Magazine* was lamenting a creeping lack of standards:

The florid style of skating shews that the fine art is disintegrating . . . we look in vain for the grand simplicity of the masters that spread-eagled in the age of its perfection.

Pl. I

FROSTIANA:
OR
A HISTORY OF
THE RIVER THAMES
In a Frozen State:

WITH AN ACCOUNT OF

THE LATE SEVERE FROST;

AND THE WONDERFUL EFFECTS
OF

Frost, Snow, Ice, and Cold,

IN ENGLAND,
AND IN DIFFERENT PARTS OF THE WORLD;

INTERSPERSED

WITH VARIOUS AMUSING ANECDOTES.

TO WHICH IS ADDED,

THE ART OF SKATING.

A dreadful winter came; each day severe,
Misty when mild, and icy-cold when clear.
                                    CRABBE.

London:

Printed and published on the ICE on the River *Thames*,
February 5th, 1814, by G. DAVIS.

Sold also by Sherwood, Neely, and Jones, Paternoster Row.

"Ice floors" first appeared in London, 1841. By 1904 the technology had reached Australia and South Africa. (New York Public Library)

The British royal family has long practiced skating—from Charles II to Charles, Prince of Wales. These are the royal skates of Victoria and Albert, 1840. (World F.S. Hall of Fame and Museum)

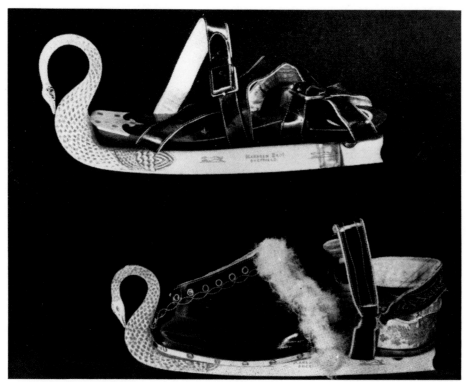

b. ALEX. LEBEDEFF 1883   f. N. PANIN 1897   g. A. CUMMING 1908

"Special figures"—once a proud feature of international competition, when skaters were master etchers. (Some are still occasionally skated in exhibitions.) One performer of fancy figures skated a love letter to his sweetheart. (World F.S. Hall of Fame and Museum)

The trouble sounds dangerously French. It's more likely, however, the complaint that comes with a growing mass interest in almost anything. "For if it be permissible to carry the unemployed leg anyhow, a wonderful diversity of kicking legs and throwing arms is seen, and who can tell how much latitude may be allowed in that direction?" warned Montague S. Monier-Williams, a Victorian expert, viewing with alarm developments of a similar stripe in his day.

Innovation and invention were in the air. Changes were coming fast. Better designed figure skates became available by 1837. "Artificial blade floors" opened by 1841. The parks were full of skaters. It was difficult to maintain standards. Figures proliferated: "The Ransom," "The Mohawk," "The Grasshopper," "The Serpentine Eight," "The Rattlesnake," "The Sea-Breeze"—to name but a few. Finally, there were hundreds. "Footprints cabalistic, algebraic," one poet called them. Continuous figures accomplished on one foot, the balance foot never touching, the body held erect, arms and free leg held close to the body, this was English skating. The figure was to be laid out and retraced perfectly by a body perfectly aligned according to rules themselves refined to perfection. "Serpentine Eight—Combining Rail Fence," "On To Richmond *Backward*," "Combined Locomotive," "Counter Rocking Turns," "Philadelphia Grapevines." "Finally, it is probably more difficult to skate in the British style than in any other, and the pleasures of over-coming difficulties is great in all true sportsmen," a spokesman defended.

The difficulty was undisputed. But some grew restless with the science of skating; they saw something else, other possibilities. And so began the endless, feckless, unresolved debate about sport and art, from which skating has yet to emerge. The defensive attitude of the English became more entrenched as the years passed by and the glory of English skating was challenged from all sides. The threat sprang from the vitality of a "sport" they had so long fostered but could no longer dominate; the loss of Empire was felt all around.

And so the skater skates through the times, drawing his continuous line through history, but only by repeating those Dutch and English loops, time and time again.

The weaker sex stands helplessly by. Colored mezzotint after painting by John Collet, 1725–1780. (World F.S. Hall of Fame and Museum)

THE SETTLERS: LEWD, RUDE, AND EXTRAVAGANT BEHAVIOR

*I*n broad outline, American skating history retraces history abroad. A sampling of some of the early entries gives some of the regional flavor.

Early Canadian records state that the Iroquois Indians chased deer across the ice on bone skates. Generic skating. We've passed this way before. . . .

Members of the DeMont expedition to Acadia (Nova Scotia) skated on the frozen ponds they found there and, according to one source, this may be the earliest record of recreational skating in all North America. It's an interesting one to ponder. The year was 1604—some sixty years before Pepys' sighting of skating in London. Was this Dutch skating on iron runners? Or some local variant of sliding on bones?

The Puritan settler in New England, of course, deplored the frivolity of sport. He "kept a copy of the King James Bible under his pillow, but he burned the King James *Book of Sport*, which openly encouraged an afternoon of recreation following divine services on Sunday," sports historian Nells Twombly writes. "That was the hated, oppressive, Anglican way, which the Puritan had sworn to destroy. And so Cotton Mather condemned 'the most abominable Impieties of Uncleanliness, Drunkeness, and a lewd, Rude, Extravagant sort of Behavior' as found in the pursuit of sport and pleasure, and then slipped away to go fishing."

"Many skaters go in the afternoon to skate upon Fresh Pond," the formidable Puritan Samuel Sewell noted, without prejudice, in his Boston Diary, November 30th, 1696. But amidst such inconsistency, one couldn't be too cautious. A school teacher was dismissed from service and charged with witchcraft for teaching young girls to skate. And it was Magistrate Samuel Sewell who passed sentence on all nineteen souls at the infamous Salem witch trials.

The Devil's work notwithstanding, it must have been difficult at best to govern men's sporting instincts. An astonished Sir Thomas Dole reportedly found half-starved colonists at Jamestown happily playing at bowls. In New Amsterdam, the Dutch Reform Church took a stern view of bowling and *kolf*—but freely permitted sleighing and skating. "The Dutch are a most unusual breed," an Englishman is quoted in Patterson's *The City of New York*. "They construct sleighs in the most fanciful fashion, some of them in the shape of swans and other water birds. They race them on the frozen ponds and they pretend that winter is not a season of cold and death. They also erect booths on the ice and spend endless hours skating and quaffing warm liquor out of pewter cups." This note of pious surprise comes, evidently, from that rare

Pages 58–59: *Skating in Central Park* by Winslow Homer, c. 1860. (St. Louis Art Museum)

Below: Special trains and trolleys jitneyed skaters to the ponds and lakes outside of Boston. Jamaica Pond, Massachusetts. (Library of Congress)

Englishman who did not revel with his countrymen in the great frost fairs of the time. Needless to say, skating continued without interruption throughout the period of British Colonial Rule. Indeed, it could not have received safer patronage. For it was Charles II who granted to his brother James much of Maine, all of Martha's Vineyard, Long Island, and a goodly portion of New Amsterdam. The skating Royals were at it again. And though the British presence eventually became insupportable to the Americans, British skating style was firmly entrenched and on display among the soldiers garrisoned near Philadelphia. Indeed, Philadelphians quickly took matters into their own hands. "Tough Philadelphians," one of these wrote, "have never reduced skating to rules like Londoners, nor connected it with their business like Dutchmen, [yet] I will hazard the opinion that they are the best and most elegant skaters in the world." Among the best certainly, as Benjamin West spontaneously demonstrated on the Serpentine. The great days of the Philadelphia skating scene were postponed until the conclusion of the Revolution. Skaters wisely leave the ice during a storm.

In 1790 only three percent of the nation's total population of four million lived in its six largest cities — Philadelphia, Boston, New York, Baltimore, Charleston — and Salem. Over half the nation, all nine hundred thousand square miles of it, was occupied by Indians. The population was so dispersed that Thomas Jefferson had to begin by trying to interest his country in the *idea* of a nation. Sixty years later, between 1840 and 1856, three million immigrants entered the port of New York; most did not move on. Three million people — a group nearly the size of the nation's total population a generation before — occupied a single city.

Suddenly, the streets were choked with people and things. Citizen Philip Hone wrote of New York in 1839, "The spirit of pulling down and building up is abroad. The whole of New York is rebuilt about once in ten years." Fellow New Yorker George Templeton Strong remarked:

Never knew the city in such a chaotic state. Every other house seems to be disgorging itself into the street, all the sidewalks are lumbered with bureaus and bedsteads to the utter destruction of their character as thoroughfares, and all the space between the sidewalks is occupied by long processions of wagons and vehicles. . . . We certainly haven't advanced as a people beyond the nomadic or migratory stage of civilization.

To suggest that city folk were feeling the stress of urban life hardly begins to tell the story, but bears on the story being told here. Relief was desperately needed from the more obscene advances of civilization. Summing it up in 1840, Nathaniel Willis remarked, "As a people we have no habit of amusement in America. Business and repose are the only states of existence we know. . . . Our health suffers from distaste for places of public relation and resort." DeTocqueville concluded ten years earlier that Americans did not "value the simple, turbulent, or coarse diversions in which people in aristocratic countries indulge." But was that really the case? It was difficult, after all, to avow that which had been forsworn. "Let no trifling diversion, or amusement . . . no girl, no gun, no cards, no flutes, no violins, no dress, no tobacco, no laziness, decoy you," John Adams had stoutly commanded himself.

But, little by little, people came to understand that the mind and body public suffered from overwork and overcrowding. The public health, indeed the public *good*, seemed at stake. And so, in a great American turnaround, expediently substituting one virtue for another, we threw open the doors and windows, raced and embraced recreation and exercise. Central Park opened in 1860 and soon the "Park Movement" began in earnest. A recreation boom started a skating boom. "Skating," enthusiast George Herbert Fowler proclaimed, "is one of the exercises the decline of which in the United States has been the primary cause of the unhealthy constitution, the pulmonary men and women, the childless wives, the dyspeptic men, the puny forms, and the bloodless cheeks which characterize the population of our great cities at the present day. . . . We are, we hope, on the right track at last. This skating business seems to have aroused public attention." It not only aroused public interest, it proved a great leveler in bringing social classes together and providing intoxicating opportunity for men and women to meet—and touch.

Exploiting the new practical philosophy toward sports and recreation, seventeen new skate patents were registered in the 1850s; one hundred forty nine were recorded in the 1860s. One retailer offered one hundred fifty varieties of ice skates through hardware stores and catalogues, priced between fifty cents and twenty-five dollars. The most elegant of clamp-on "Club skates" were made of tooled steel and packed like dueling pistols in a velvet-lined case.

At these prices nearly everyone could afford skates of some kind—or the price of a rental for a day's outing. With the opening of Central Park in 1860 daily crowds of fifty thousand packed into the park for skating. In Boston, fifteen hundred passengers were shuttling between the city and the outlying ponds. America was quickly drawing abreast of the skating craze in England. Whereas thirty-four hundred

By mid-nineteenth century, the ponds of Central Park in New York City were thick with skaters—50,000 a day during a hard freeze. (Harper's Weekly, 1860)

By 1868, covered rinks were everywhere. New York featured a rink the size of a football field. (The Bettmann Archive)

Below: Stern measures for ladies with weak ankles. Brass ankle supports and trim, c. 1860. (World F.S. Hall of Fame and Museum)

Opposite: Cutlery for the feet: from a skate-maker's catalog, nineteenth century. One catalog offered over one hundred models. Prices ranged from $.25 to $25. (Library of Congress)

people might be seen skating upon the twenty acres of ice at Wimbledon Lake, one hundred seventy groundsmen, a term still respectfully associated with Wimbledon, diligently cared for the ice in a storm.

London established its first skating club in 1830 with the patronage of the Prince of Wales and the Duke of Cambridge. America answered with its first skating club in 1850, The Philadelphia Skating Club and Humane Society, a scene of rather a different sort.

Skating, as we know, had long been popular in and around Philadelphia. The Schuykill River made for wonderful skating with ice two feet thick (before steamboats came along and ruined everything). Here was the training ground of Benjamin West and "the Philadelphia prodigies" the English so admired a century earlier. And there were other well-known personalities of the time. "William Thorpe, Doctor Faulke, Governor Mifflin, Charles Wilson Peale, George Heyl, and a negro named Joe Claypoole who wore 'low-gutter skates' and was particularly swift in his movements. George Heyl . . . was especially graceful and clever at figure skating, and dressed, as was then the fashion, in a red coat and buckskin tights," according to J. F. Lewis, writing in 1895. Doctor Faulke, a famous local surgeon, was appropriately adept at cutting his own name into the ice—and executing a move called the "High Dutch." Governor Mifflin was a merchant, statesman, member of the Continental Congress and *aide-de-campe* to General George Washington. Charles Wilson Peale, also an officer in the Revolution, was, of course, the well-known portrait painter.

In the years that followed, the skating public grew in size. The skating club was formed for "the instruction and improvement in the art of skating, the cultivation of a friendly feeling in all who participate in the amusement, [and] the efficient use of proper apparatus for the rescue of persons breaking through the ice." People were falling through the ice, it seems, with alarming regularity. By 1853, twenty-eight lives had been saved by the good people of the Philadelphia Skating Club. By 1859, one hundred twenty-five more souls had been saved. Henceforth, they added to their name the designation "Humane Society." A humorous accommodation since more lives were being risked and saved due to skating than to any other peril. Club rescuers skated with a reel and sixty feet of cord ending in a noose that was slipped over the rescuer's wrist. The reel was then thrown to the victim. Safety ladders of light wood with a hundred feet of rope were also used, as well as boats on runners, danger flags, ropes to mark air holes and weak spots, life preservers, boat hooks and grappling irons. Skating in Pennsylvania, it would seem, was not for the faint-hearted. A period remedy for overexertion (a New York recipe) called for:

The Philadelphia Skating Club and the Humane Society joined forces for practical reasons: one hand always seemed to be reaching for the other. (World F.S. Hall of Fame and Museum)

8 oz. fat of stag or deer

6 oz. Florence oil (or olive)

3 oz. white wax

1 grain musk

½ pint brandy

4 oz. rose water

The instructions were to place the fat, oil, and wax in an earthen vessel and simmer over a low fire, then to add the remaining ingredients and let cool until ready. Mercifully, you did not have to drink the stuff—just rub it on your stiffened joints.

After the opening of the Philadelphia club, between 1863 (the year New York established its first Skating Club) and 1867, nine more skating clubs opened in Philadelphia. By 1868 they had an indoor rink—as did Chicago, St. Louis, Cincinnati, Cleveland, Pittsburg, Quincy (Massachusetts), Springfield (Illinois), Indianapolis, Columbus, Buffalo, Rochester, Syracuse, Oswego, Boston, Brooklyn, and Jersey City. One such rink, the "Empire City" in New York, at 63rd and Third Avenue, was three hundred fifty feet long, one hundred seventy feet wide: a football field of ice lit with seven hundred gas burners.

Skating clubs opened both at home and abroad in quick succession like fast food franchises. *The Cercle de Patineurs* (with the noble patronage of Le Marquis de Mornay, Le Prince Murat, Le Marquis de Castelbajac, etc.) was established in 1865 for skating in the *Bois*. In Russia the Neva Skating Association preceded them by a year in St. Petersburg. The Vienna *Eislaufverein* followed in 1867. The skating boom had turned into an international skating movement. The next question was inevitable: which skater, which country, was the best?

Ladies' costume while suitable for "figures" greatly restricted their ability to jump and spin. Change in fashion liberated women as freestylists. Illustration by C. H. Kuechler, 1895. (Mary Evans Picture Library)

Jackson Haines, the first great celebrity skater. (National Museum of Finland, Helsinki)

THE INTERNATIONAL STYLE: SKATING AS SPECTACLE

They say that just before a performance he dipped his blades in boiling water, then rushed on to the ice, spinning. The people loved him. Special rinks were built for him when he came to skate. Babies and perfumes were named after him. Women clamored for just a glimpse, tearing at the canvas around the rink for a peek. He was an international celebrity the equal of Caruso or Jenny Lind. His name was Jackson Haines. He was received in the most brilliant circles—Paris, Vienna, Prague, Moscow, St. Petersburg, Stockholm, Helsinki. He was adored by royalty. Emperor Franz Joseph was his admirer, Czar Alexander his student. No one had ever seen his like before.

Imagine you're in Vienna in 1866. Put yourself in mind of a waltz. Dipping, whirling, circles of three-four time that won't stop. Waltz after waltz. Each one is different, each is the same: delightful, deranged. One two-three, one two-three. The whole city is waltzing. Now imagine a foreigner, an American, inviting the city to come dancing on the ice. And for the first time, a man sweeps up to a woman, blades flashing, bows, takes her in his arms, and suddenly they are a pair, dancing, sweeping, gliding over the ice.

Skating in pairs, dancing on ice, Jackson Haines started it all. And more. Skates of his own design bolted to the boot. Bolder figures designed on a larger axis, yet intricate as Valencienne lace. Everything preplanned, set to music, choreographed in delicate sketches.

History has a way of turning up the right man in the right place at the right moment. Vienna, a city that honored Johann Strauss at his death by parading through the streets with his violin—strings slashed—on a velvet pillow, had nothing to fear from a young man full of music and dance.

In America, Haines had been proclaimed "champion" in 1863—but where, or by whom, or for what, isn't clear. It is clear, however, that people in eastern skating circles didn't care for his skating "exhibitions." They found his style posy and affected. Americans liked their skating forthright—fast, tricked-out, accurate. Haines had other ideas.

Ice skating, over the years, had become immensely popular. It had mass appeal and accessibility; all it needed now was a hero. Haines embodied all that skating was and could be. He made the pulse flutter, the heart leap. He liberated, by his own example, imagination and aspiration in others. He possessed the vision, daring, excellence, and nimbus to fill the role, and he had the wit to live and die like a legend as well. But America was not ready for the skating king.

It is said Jackson Haines was born in 1840 to Alexander Frazee Haines and Elizabeth Terhune Earl (he of English descent, she of Dutch — the appropriate lineage for a skater) in New York. He was also alleged to have been born in Boston, Chicago, Troy, Albany, and Canada. Haines died at thirty-five, thirty-six, sometime in his thirties, in January of 1875, in June of 1876, from exposure in a sleigh crossing Russia, in an attic from pneumonia.

He was one of five children. His father was — a successful businessman, a hat-maker, a cabinet-maker, possibly a grocer. Young Haines was sent to "select schools" where he received special tutoring in French, music, and dance. He was taken to Europe at the age of ten in the care of a relative, in the care of a guardian. He remained "there" for seven years during which time he studied ballet. At seventeen he returned to America and drove a truck, "trained for a theatrical career," studied dance in New York, became a dancing master, did an Indian-club act in a variety show. Early on he married Alma Bogart, daughter of a Judge Abram Bogart of New York. They had two sons, Eugene and Abram, and a daughter, Clara. At some time he became a Freemason.

According to a Finnish newspaper clipping, Haines' parents "wanted him to become a well-to-do businessman. He was put to work in an office . . . but the ice skating rink pulled him with an irresistible force. The office floor burned his feet made to carry skates. Haines made a name in Boston and New York where he soon outdid every young member of these cities' skating clubs."

There is, in fact, no record that he was a member of either club, for the very good reason that both the Boston and Cambridge Skating Clubs formed after his death. He is referred to, at this time, as the "Canadian" and "American Champion." But again, the details regarding these honors are vague. Safe to say, he was recognized but his innovations were not encouraged. In 1864 Haines left his wife and children and traveled abroad to seek his fortune and make his reputation. He never returned to America again.

Not quite twenty-four, Jackson Haines appeared in London at The Alhambra; next, in Paris, on a pair of roller skates in a production of Meyerbeer's *La Prophète;* then in Stockholm where he was received, at last, as an *artiste.* In 1866 came his triumphs in Vienna. Newspaper accounts gushed, reviews glowed, money and medals were bestowed. For the next eleven years, under conditions and over terrain that are nearly unimaginable to us now, he traveled the length and breadth of northern Europe. Reviewing his career and influence, *The New York Times* reported, "He went to Vienna to further dance study and remained to electrify not alone the people of that city but all Europe as well by his eleven years of brilliant performance,

Considered too "artsy" by American standards, Jackson Haines triumphed abroad on both rollers and blades. (National Museum of Finland, Helsinki)

not as an indoor dancer but as a figure skater. . . . From his style of skating, supplely erect, not stiff, limbs free and flowing in graceful carriage, always in balance in the middle or forward portion of his skating edge rather than on the back portion used by all other skaters of his time, he developed the now accepted 'International Style,' which had been used by all good skaters from his time down to the present."

Yet he could have been anyone. Look at his face—past the proud held pose of early photography, the piercing eyes told not to blink, see the small unremarkable features. He could have been Billy the Kid. He could have been a banker. What he had done, in fact, was dance on the ice to the music of Bellini, Verdi, and Strauss. He dressed up as a lady, he dressed up as a polar bear and a Savoyard. He did everything from pratfalls to pirouettes—fused in music, theater, choreography. He made people want to skate, and want to do it his way. All artistic and figure skating owes this man an incalculable debt. And, as one notable skater observed, "He was a prophet without honor in his own country."

Jackson Haines died of pneumonia in Gamla-Karleby, Finland, on June 23, 1875, the eve of summer. He'd lost touch with his wife and had been notified, on tour, of the drowning deaths in the Hudson River of his two young sons. It is hinted that a love affair brought him to the remote coastal village where he died. He is buried in the local churchyard. There his headstone is inscribed with these punishing words from *Ecclesiastes:* "For there is no work, nor device, nor knowledge, nor wisdom, in the grave, whither thou goest."

＊　　　　＊　　　　＊

Wherever Jackson Haines appeared there followed a phenomenal surge of interest in skating. In some places it happened for the first time. But, more astonishingly, he is credited with having revived, single-handedly, a natural passion for skating in Scandinavia. Skating clubs sprang up everywhere. In Vienna the *Eislaufverein* was the first of these to build an instructional program in the Haines or International Style. All at once, the entrenched American and English styles were being threatened from abroad. Where skating had once been practiced as something of a science, it was now being presented as spectacle, something to see.

By the 1890s the skating world was becoming well organized at the local, national, and international

Jackson Haines, darling of royalty, gave lessons to Czar Alexander II. Self-invented and self-made, father of modern freestyle skating, he lived and died mysteriously—as legends should. His grave site is at Gamla-Karleby, Finland. (World F.S. Hall of Fame and Museum)

levels. And there was great interest in competition. The first "international skating meeting" was held in Vienna in 1882. The program consisted of *twenty-three* compulsory figures (Olympians complain today about the three figures assigned), a special figure chosen and traced by each competitor, and a four-minute free-skating program. The winner of this first international meet was appropriately a student of Jackson Haines, Leopold Frey. Third place was awarded to a Norwegian, Axel Paulsen, who displayed on this same occasion the jump of one-and-one-half revolutions that bears his name and has plagued skaters ever since.

Little by little, the International Style found acceptance and prevailed. An English woman named Madge Syers, an early convert to the International Style, entered the conventionally all-male World Championship and finished second to Ulrich Salchow, the reigning world champion. The contest was instantly closed to women ever after; a separate event was established for them instead. Ms. Syers won the first Olympic ladies' singles title in 1908. Salchow went on to amass the greatest skating record of any male skater in history, defending the World title ten times, the European title nine times, and winning the first Olympic men's singles title in 1908. He attempted to defend his title in 1920 (World War I canceled the interceding Olympic Games) but was beaten by a younger man—Gillis Grafstrom of Sweden. Salchow finished second in the figures, fourth overall, at the age of 42.

Grafstrom became widely regarded as the finest "interpretive" skater of the modern era. Envied for his control and flexibility and a marvelous "softness" of knee, he became famous as a stylist and inventor of new patterns and positions, among them the flying sit spin, the inside spiral, and assorted combinations of steps, spins, and jumps.

America, in the meantime, had not had a close look at the International Style since the 1860s when Haines had decamped for Europe. So it took the determined interest of two Americans, Irving Brokaw and George Browne, to go abroad and import that which had been exported in the first place. The conversion of these two passionate skaters to the International Style resulted in exhibition and exhortation beginning in 1908 that would eventually have everyone convinced as to which way the future lay. Brokaw, a wealthy New Yorker and prime mover in the St. Nicholas Skating Club, was himself the American Champion in 1906. "To go through the American Championship programme of 1906," he wrote, "I had to skate a full ½ hour on threes alone, and another ½ hour on spins. It made for endurance and stamina, of nothing else. But it

Page 78 left: Madge Syers of Great Britain came in second to the great Ulrich Salchow at the World Championship, 1902. A separate ladies event was hastily established. (World F.S. Hall of Fame and Museum)

Page 78 right: Ulrich Salchow of Sweden amassed the greatest skating record of any male skater in history, and secured the first Olympic men's gold medal, 1908. (World F.S. Hall of Fame and Museum)

Page 79 left and right: National Swedish, World, and Olympic champion, Gillis Grafstrom possessed an Astaire-like elegance rarely seen in men's skating. (World F.S. Hall of Fame and Museum)

Opposite right: Andrée Joly and Pierre Brunet, of France. Early pair champions and Olympic gold medalists, 1928, 1932. (World F.S. Hall of Fame and Museum)

Opposite left: Irving Brokaw. (Library of Congress)

———

utterly lacked grace, beauty of carriage, rhythm, and the long flowing curves inseparably connected with the sweeping strokes on ice. As an artist I rebelled against the cramped restricted style."

The weight of Brokaw's accomplishments as a skater, along with his social influence in skating circles, did much to bring about the change. At his canny suggestion, American producer Charles Dillingham engaged German skating star "Charlotte" (last name Oelschlagel)—Europe's most bewitching exponent of the International Style—to appear at the Hippodrome, then the largest playhouse in America. The plan was to run six weeks. The show in which she starred, "Flirting in St. Moritz," opened in 1915, played twice a day to six thousand people, and closed three years later. A peak moment for some was her skating of the "Dying Swan" performed in tandem with Anna Pavlova. Others remember, can't forget, the star's incredible long hair free-flowing to her ankles. Suffice it to say, the International Style was a stunning success with the American public. Serious and amateur skaters gathered eagerly between the shows for impromptu instruction and demonstration on the semi-permanent ice floor fondly nicknamed "Lake Moritz."

That same year, Charlotte appeared in *The Frozen Warning*, the first ice-skating movie, directed by an associate of D. W. Griffith, Oscar Eagle. It was a silent thriller about World War I espionage. The plot turned on Miss Oelschlagel's ability to trace the word S-P-I-E-S on the ice, thereby warning her endangered and completely unsuspecting countrymen. (There have been sillier plots to more pretentious movies. Indeed, it sounds like early Hitchcock. No matter, the public liked it well enough.) The stage was now set for Sonja Henie, whose popularity went virtually unrivaled in the decade she made her eleven movies—between 1936 and 1948.

One in a Million, Countess of Monte Cristo, Thin Ice, Sun Valley Serenade, were some of the titles. Her skating, by present-day standards, seems lady-like, pleasant. Acting certainly wasn't her event. But the production numbers are fun, if you like that sort of thing. And people did. Miss Henie made a personal fortune of more than forty-seven million dollars from her films alone. The lady had glamour, star quality,

―――――――

and she could actually do something. The ritual revealing of her talent as the narrative unfolded never lost its appeal. This was no helpless ninny, no tinsel goddess. This girl could skate. Really skate. She was the-best-skater-in-the-whole-world. And she could prove it. Sonja Henie turned ice skating into big business. There was something about her proven ability all packaged Hollywood style that made her—and ice skating—unbelievably popular. Suddenly, there was ice everywhere: ice rinks, ice shows, ice extravaganzas of every kind, mini-rinks in night clubs and on top of hotels—the entertainment boom was on.

While the media were, by no means, as enmeshed as they are now, newspapers, magazines, newsreels, movies, and radio certainly could make careers. Sonja Henie was a public figure from the time she was a little girl. Born in Norway in 1913, she entered—and won—her first skating contest at the age of 7. She entered her first international contest at 11. By 14, the World title was hers. She defended it successfully, and annually, for the next ten years. Then there were the three consecutive gold medal wins at the Olympics. No other woman in any sport has ever achieved that. Meanwhile, she was European Ladies Champion for six years running. She retired as a competitor in 1936, and that same year tried her hand at movies. One senses her public had grown up with her and wanted her success.

While her personal ambition and business acumen may not have endeared her to the competition, she set a standard of performance and presentation that simply had to be met or bettered. As an athlete, she was admired for her strength, consistency, and spins. As an artist, she had fluidity and elegance. As an entertainer, she had no equal. The amateur competition never stood a chance. While they toiled away in baggy tights and droopy black skirts, Miss Henie displayed a wardrobe of the most elegant costumes, many of them designed by Worth of Paris. She wore jewels to practice, eschewed black boots and switched to white. She was also the first to wear short skirts; some would say that was a declaration of war. Others have been more charitable: Miss Henie skated that way as a child and she never made the switch. Perhaps. What is important is that she set a style which liberated all women to skate freer and more athletic programs. The results were immediate: women began to jump and spin as they never had—or could—before.

Dick Button is perhaps the only other modern skater whose influence could be said to rival that of Sonja Henie. Entering his first competition at 13 and placing second, he never won less than a gold medal in any United States or Sectional Championship he entered thereafter. In 1948 he became the first skater from the United States to win the Olympic men's title which he successfully defended in 1952 while enrolled at

Sonja Henie at age 16. She held more skating titles than any woman before or since. (The Bettmann Archive)

The great Sonja Henie. Norwegian, World, and Olympic champion, 1927-36. She finessed the competition with ability, dimples, and a wardrobe that put the other girls to shame. (The Bettmann Archive)

Dick Button, five times World champion, two times Olympic gold medalist, and winner of the "grand slam" in 1948—sweeping every title in the world. (Dick Button Collection)

Canadian, North American, World, and European champion—Barbara Ann Scott of Canada in 1948 became the first North American to win an Olympic gold medal. (World F.S. Hall of Fame and Museum)

Alexsei Ulanov and Irina Rodnina, four times Soviet Union World pairs champions, Olympic gold medalists, 1972.
(World F.S. Hall of Fame and Museum)

Page 88 left: Tenley Albright, first United States Ladies Olympic gold medalist, 1956. (World F.S. Hall of Fame and Museum)

Page 88 right: Carol Heiss, United States Olympic gold medalist, 1960. (World F.S. Hall of Fame and Museum)

Page 89 left: John Curry of Great Britain swept the National, European, World, and Olympic titles in 1976—and set a new standard for artistic excellence in men's singles skating. (Margaret S. Williamson)

Page 89 right: Cubist arabesques, body slides across the ice, 1976 Canadian Olympic bronze medalist Toller Cranston created a new vocabulary of movement and gave freestyle new dramatic license. (Margaret S. Williamson)

———

Harvard as an honors student. Five times World Champion, three times North American Champion, and seven times United States Champion, Button was, along with Barbara Ann Scott of Canada, the first—and last—North American to win the European Championship; it was promptly closed to non-Europeans thereafter. Widely regarded as the father of modern free skating, Button was the first skater to perform in competition a double Axel, three consecutive toe triple loops, and a flying camel spin. His triple loop jump at the Olympics still stands as a record. No skater has successfully pulled off a "Quad"—yet. But they're working on it.

If these technical terms evade you, you could not have been listening. Or watching. Dick Button, with the enthusiasm of a gifted teacher and the patience of a diplomat, has single-handedly been tutoring a worldwide audience in the fine points of competitive skating for over twenty years. If we show any promise of being a more discerning audience, it is because we have watched skating through Dick Button's intelligent eyes.

A procession of remarkable skaters has glided past in the intervening years. It's good to remember some of their names: Hayes Alan Jenkins and his brother David; Tenley Albright; Carol Heiss; Peggy Fleming; Dorothy Hamill; the Protopopovs; Irina Rodnina and her husbands (Ulanov then Zaitzev); Tai Babilonia and Randy Gardner; Judy Blumberg and Michael Seibert; Janet Lynn; Toller Cranston; John Curry; Robin Cousins; Jayne Torvill and Christopher Dean.

We have passed through a long period of athleticism in skating (children are executing the triple jumps Dick Button introduced in adult competition). At its best, it has been breakneck and breathtaking; at its worst, a tired exhibition of the disco self.

Change comes slowly in a wary, entrenched skating establishment. Toller Cranston offended at first with his deviant style, at once bizarre and balletic. Too flashy. John Curry was criticized for his slow velvet stroking of the ice, a technique restrained by the twin demands of music and choreography. Where were the tricks? Too artsy.

Yet Cranston and Curry have proved to be, without question, the most influential endurance skaters of the present era. As a performer, Cranston has been imitated by dozens of young skaters. The surreal extensions, cubist arabesques, body slides across the ice—all are quotes from Cranston. Curry's

Society back on the ice again. Tuxedo, New York. (Library of Congress)

Four centuries of ice skating continues in New York, with a little help from Donald Trump. The renovated Wollman Memorial Rink, 1987. (The New York Times, photo by Keith Meyers)

influence, by comparison, is subtler and, in its way, more subversive as it questions the conventions of training and performance—reaching past competition to the skater's most personal reasons for dedicating a lifetime to such discipline.

*   *   *

For centuries, skating has continued to be the excited natural reaction to a hard frost, as surely as sledding follows a good snowfall. Outdoor skating, skating to the weather, is like dancing to the music; it just seems to be in us to do it. Part of this kind of skating is waiting, waiting for winter, waiting for the temperature to drop and stay there, seeing a thin skin of ice form—waiting for it to thicken and bear—then having it happen. It's an experience that can't be cheapened, and there's no way to improve on it.

No one has to wait for a freeze to skate, of course. Indoor skating is available year round, as it has been since the latter part of the nineteenth century, when the first ice parlors opened in London and skaters found themselves gliding through an indoor fog lifting romantically off an uncertain recipe for ice.

As cities proliferated and grew larger, rivers, ponds, and lakes became compromised, less accessible, and so modern man took his skating indoors. And gradually, with adaptation, came transformation, the breeding of a new type, the modern indoor skater. Indoor skating is by definition more confined, some would say less sporting and spontaneous. Somehow, without the distractions and intrusions of nature, the skater seems more thrown in upon himself; the skating becomes all about skating.

This transition from outdoor to indoor skating is so complete by now that when we speak of skating it's generally assumed we're talking about someone, or something, seen indoors. It goes further than that. Television has bred a whole new genus of enthusiasts—non-participant skaters—graduates, so to speak, of the Dick Button School of Television Commentary. There is, for the first time, a generation of interested, intelligent observers who count skating among their cultivated interests, yet do not skate a stroke. Their developed appreciation of fine skating could well produce a skating aesthetic that will carry skating into its future. We already know that skating changes, and changes with the times. The transitions create odd effects: skaters, for example, who have never competed on outdoor ice. Many express a horror of frozen ponds and rivers. Champion John Curry, experienced at both conditions, recalls a nightmare of falling through the ice and seeing it open and close, open and close, like a revolving door overhead. Still, remembering the joys of outdoor skating, he is known to slip onto the ice at Rockefeller Center's pond in New York City just before closing, to feel the night air, see the skyline wheeling past, and for those moments he embodies all of skating—past, present, and future.

Once the technology for rink ice became universally available, competitors lost all patience with skating figures in a stiff wind or puddle. In 1967, the International Skating Union (ISU) finally moved to bring international competition indoors. Too much time, money, effort, talent, and national interest was riding on the competitors' performances to risk accidents and delays. This, nearly a century after the invention of artificial rink ice; the skating establishment is nothing if not conservative. Indeed, skating is an enterprise in which seniors remain actively, and influentially involved. Many veteran skaters administrate and judge in the national skating program. Some of these view change with a notorious degree of skepticism. Certain gentlewomen and gentlemen, still skating in their eighties, remember Miss Henie and Mr. Grafstrom in competition, blades clattering over rough and melting ice at St. Moritz, the Alps rising fiercely in the distance, and they'll tell you that something is lost when you bring an outdoor sport indoors, put a lid on it. Real champions, they say, meet every kind of challenge—blinding sun and snow, thin mountain air, gusting winds. Modern champions would answer that they meet all the challenges—and then some: costly year-round training programs, heavy schedules of competition and exhibition, jet travel. While technology may smooth and maintain the ice, each new miracle asserts its own demands. Gone are the long, healing ocean voyages between international competitions, the ice-free months without training, the poor performances remembered only in the local press. New hazards abound, both physical and psychological: bodies, minds, growth, pushed beyond natural limits. Such stories plague every highly contested modern sport. Yet, despite the excesses and changes, the continuing marvel of skating history is that nothing is lost to progress. Skating exists in all its forms simultaneously. The hot young competitor trains at the modern Boston Skating Club while an elderly couple waltzes across open ice at the historic Cambridge Skating Club—a rink flooded by a garden hose. A half mile north, a lone skater steals across acres of natural ice at Fresh Pond. Minutes away, children test new skates and new ice at Spy Pond where skating has continued uninterrupted for three hundred winters.

Skating in Central Park by Agnes Tait, 1934. (National Museum of American Art)

Indoor ice rink, the Williams Center, Tulsa, Oklahoma. (Photo: Alvis Upitis/The Image Bank)

HOCKEY: A DISORDERLY MOB, ARMED WITH STICKS

The close of the nineteenth century brought with it the last significant evolutionary moment in skating—the beginnings of modern ice hockey. Thwack! Crunching, lunging, smashing—the hockey players take the ice. From a London newspaper, 1862:

Hockey . . . ought to be sternly forbidden, as it is not only annoying (to leisurely skaters on a pond) but dangerous. . . . When a mass of human beings precipitates itself recklessly in any direction, accidents are sure to follow. . . . The game is by no means what it ought to be, as it is impossible to enforce the rules in such a miscellaneous assembly. . . . It is more than annoying to have the graceful evolutions of a charming quadrille broken up by the interruptions of a disorderly mob, armed with sticks and charging through the circle of skaters and spectators to the imminent danger of all. I should be truly glad to see the police interfere whenever hockey is commenced.

The modern origins of both the name of the game and game of that name are in dispute, but, there are ancient carvings that suggest the Greeks played some variant of field hockey as early as 500 B.C. The English have played what is recognizably field hockey for centuries. The Dutch started an ice game in the seventeenth century akin to hockey called kolven. The Irish played their variant and called it hurling or hurley. The Canadian-Indian game of baggataway, or lacrosse, has its parallels but shinny, as it was played in the northeastern United States, appears to be the true antecedent. The object of the game was to control the ball, or a bit of wood, with a stick and shoot it between stones set a few feet apart. In time, the game was moved out on the ice. "I can hear the roar of the runners yet," a piece from *Outing* magazine reads, dated 1913, "and see the white powder fly as the leader doubled and the whole pack ground their blades into the ice and reversed in pursuit. . . . The boys are at it yet, though they all have 'store sticks' now, and call the game hockey."

How they came to name it is unclear. One story has it that a band of Iroquois Indians was seen by some French explorers "whacking with sticks at a hard ball and reacting to certain misdirected blows by shouting 'Ho-gee!'" ("it hurts!"). The year was 1740. This entirely plausible explanation is shunned by scholars who insist that the word derives from *hoquet*, French for shepherd's crook, or bent stick.

The English claim an early form of ice hockey played in the middle 1800s, the Americans boast of their own primitive experiments, but it is the Canadians who have made the loudest and most passionate claim—insisting that the rules of modern hockey are Canadian—assertions they will cheerfully back up

Page 96: United States hockey team, 1980 Olympics—at the end of the game. (Photo: Heinz Kluetmeier/Sports Illustrated)

Top: A seventeenth-century Dutch event—jumping salt barrels. (The Bettmann Archive)

Bottom: Sail-skating, skate-sailing, wind-assisted locomotion is an ancient variant. Modern skates are often fashioned from hacksaws for durability over rough ice at speeds exceeding 50 mph. (The Bettmann Archive)

Kolf, an early Dutch game akin to hockey. R. de Hooge, c. 1790–1810. (World F.S. Hall of Fame and Museum)

Possibly American, probably Canadian, even the historical roots of hockey are hotly disputed.
(Photo: © Clemens Kalischer)

with shepherd's crooks. And so the records generally agree that sometime in the 1880s ice hockey emerged in a form roughly equivalent to that being played today; the rules of conduct are said to have been invented by students at McGill University. What is certain is that hockey, by this time, is as undeniably Canadian as canal skating is Dutch.

Should ice hockey be included in a discussion of the fine art of skating, or is it merely an upstart branch to be shunned? Everything depends upon perspective, the angle of vision. The point of view here is merely evolutionary, which explains why the further history of ice hockey, down to the present, is conveniently left to the record books. While great teams and personalities have emerged and prevailed, rules and equipment have been modified, professional and Olympic competition have commanded world attention, the skating remains fundamentally the same—and a means to an end at that. The same can be said of sail-skating and barrel-jumping; compound skating that has endured, virtually unchanged, for centuries. Speed skating, a sport as old as the second pair of skates, exists almost by itself in a pure and timeless form. Figure skating alone seems to seek and find *new* forms; perhaps that is because it is about form.

COMPETITORS: THE BEST AND THE REST

S ome are just learning to skate, some are skating better this year than last. A few seem born to it. Who *are* these people? Ask an expert. John Misha Petkevich, two-time Olympic competitor, lists as indispensable the ability to manage physical feats easily, capability for rapid motion, power over the full range of movement, and being "at one with the ice." He would know, of course. Still, it seems more a description of manifest accomplishment than latent capability. We want to know: what's he got we haven't got? Writer Laurie Lee understands:

This magic substance, with its deceptive surface, was something I could never master. It put wings on my heels and gave me the motions of Mercury, then threw me down on my nose. Yet it chose its own darlings, never the ones you supposed, the dromedary louts of the schoolroom, who came skating past with one leg in the air, who twirled and simpered and darted like swifts; and never fell—not they.

—*Cider With Rosie* by Laurie Lee

"It's own darlings"—one barbed remark and we have the whole picture, the awful truth about their possibilities and our limitations. The complainer touches on something important: the "chosen" seem to possess, in common and apart, a distinct and powerful axis which renders fundamental balance and timing a delight instead of a struggle. You see it straight off in the skating, there's motor pleasure in it. And seeing the thing done right feels right to the observer, gives a measure of surrogate satisfaction that fulfills, for that moment, our own longing for balance and beauty. This axis is sometimes detected in skaters so young and so light they barely leave a tracing on the ice. "I think it might be wise," one expert, Robert Ogilvie, has written, "to put a child on the ice at the age of two or three . . . and, when he has learned to skate forward and backward quite happily, take him off for a couple of seasons; then, at about five or six, put him back on the ice in a class situation." "Balance," he adds, "acquired at a very early age seems to be more refined than that learned later in life." Starting out early has its practical advantages too. As someone once pointed out, we have less dignity to lose—and not as far to fall. The infant success of Janet Lynn is often mentioned in this connection. Miss Lynn began skating soon after she mastered walking, and having mastered skating, started winning shortly after that. She later took an Olympic title and established, in her skating, truly a timeless standard of beauty and excellence; it's the perfect example. There is, of course, the case of the chubby little New Jersey boy who could not be dissuaded from skating though his body was all wrong for it. Anyone looking at little Richard Toten Button could see the problem—too stocky, too muscular—no future there.

While not all recreational skaters begin or develop as prodigiously as these two, it is not unusual for skaters to develop on their own to a most unusual degree—just for the satisfaction it brings—and to remain actively, ardently, involved in the sport late into life. "You may have seen my mother," novelist John Cheever writes, "waltzing on ice skates in Rockefeller Center. She's seventy-eight years old now," he continues, uneasily:

She wears a red velvet costume with a short skirt. Her tights are flesh colored, and she wears spectacles and a red ribbon in her white hair, and she waltzes with one of the attendants. I don't know why I should find the fact that she waltzes on skates so disconcerting, but I do. I avoid that neighborhood whenever I can during the winter months, and I never lunch in the restaurants on the rink. Once when I was passing that way, a total stranger took me by the arm and said, "Look at that crazy old dame. . . ."

Powerful stroking, sharp edges, good position, nice moves, are becoming to skaters of all ages and describe the best of the skating we see in public places. Occasionally, if we're lucky, some one of these skaters will break loose from the circling crowd and show something more—speeding, spinning, jumping—and we glimpse what skating *can* be. Here is the skating of amateur competitors, something we're rarely privileged to see except at peak moments of international competition or, after the fact, as packaged entertainment, when the amateur turns professional.

What about *them*? Who are *these* people? Books answer the wrong question. We don't want to know "how to," we want to know "what's it like?"

*   *   *

Amateur competitors skate at rinks like the rest of us, but they come on the ice at odd hours, before sunup and after sundown, to avoid the crowds; they need plenty of ice.

They pull on their skates like anyone else—except they wear theirs out, as many as three pairs a year. And they don't lace theirs up in that deliberate way we do, yanking and cleating, yanking and cleating, but

"Show me something you think is beautiful." John Curry, to his very young pupil, Katherine Healey. With a double career in ballet, she developed outside the established competitive structure. (Margaret S. Williamson)

with a quick whipping action that finishes while we're still stabbing the first eyelet with the wet end of an old lace.

And they certainly don't wear three pairs of socks to keep warm. Some skate barefoot, to "feel" the edges; for those who wear socks, silk is preferred.

As for the skates themselves, respectable combination models—boots and blades—sell for as little as $40. Competitors pay as much as $300—just for the boots—which come in a variety of models: something soft for figures, something solid for freestyle, another both solid and flexible for dance. What with heavy use, growing feet, and skating more than one event, skaters learn to economize. A pair of wilting freestyle boots can be substituted for outgrown figure skating boots which, in turn, can be handed down to a more junior skater looking for a bargain.

Bargain blades sell for as little as $12 but they're no economy, experts say. Cheap blades are not made of steel hard enough to run well on the ice and they do not sharpen properly (blades are sharpened to suit both the event and the skater). The skater with poor equipment can't execute properly and, blaming himself, may resort to extra lessons and ice time which can prove very costly indeed. Top competitors, requiring easily as much of their blades as fencers and chefs, insist on top quality. Again, these may cost as much as $300. These also come in a variety of models which, while not interchangeable, are adaptable—with modifications. Design features address matters of toe picks, width of blade, curvature end to end (called *radius*), and length. Toe picks are what children use to tip-toe over to the hot chocolate counter. Their intended use, however, is to keep you from falling over frontwards while you are skating backwards. They also assist in launching jumps, pivoting, and in some of the fancy footwork. Pairs and freestylists use accentuated picks, dancers and skaters of figures like them minimized and set higher on the blade to avoid tripping. The distinctions go on: dancers use the thinnest blades to achieve grip with minimal friction, figures require the flattest blade to make a long, steady run. Freestylists work with a shorter curved blade to facilitate spins—yet sufficiently long to land jumps safely. Further refinements, achieved through sharpening, contour the hollow in the blade, reducing or accentuating the bite of the edges, as needed. Where the weekend skater might attend to sharpening once a year, the competitor sees his trusted sharpener once a month (the competitive skater can literally loose his edge through bungled sharpening).

Opposite left: An unexpected pair—two Olympian soloists: Robin Cousins (1980) and Peggy Fleming (1968). (Margaret S. Williamson)

Opposite right: Two of the many great California skating champions. Tai Babilonia and Randy Gardner, 1980 United States Olympic pairs team. (Margaret S. Williamson)

Those of you with a head for figures will already have guessed the bad news: competitive skating is expensive. Champion Petkevich estimates the overall expenses of the "recreational" skater to be a little over $1,000 a year for lessons, ice time, equipment, etc. Top competitors are looking at $10,000 to $50,000 a year. This does not include affiliated expenses to the families of skaters, of course. Wear and tear on the family car (not to mention the family), relocation, etc. How families provide for their exceptional children is a continuing mystery and inspiration. "I owe everything in my career," one skater writes in the dedication of her book, "to my dear sweet silent mother and understanding Daddy-Daddy who sat home patiently and paid the bills." You too might fall silent with expenses like these:

Ice time (four hours per day, six days per week, forty weeks per year)	$4,800
Instruction (eight lessons per week)	4,800
Off-ice instruction (six hours per week, forty weeks per year)	1,200
Equipment (three pairs of skates per year)	1,200
Other equipment	100
Costumes and practice outfits	1,500
Music	200
Makeup and props	100
Publicity photographs	300
Dues and fees	500
Tutors (for classes in skills missed because of competitions, or because of preparation for competition)	500
Competition expenses: skater	2,000
Competition expenses: coach	1,500
Special foods and dietary supplements	1,000
Parents' expenses for travel (at this level of competition, the USFSA Memorial Fund generally takes care of the skater's travel expenses)	5,000
Miscellaneous expenses	1,000
Total	$25,700

(With permission, *The Skater's Handbook*, John Misha Petkevich, Scribner's, New York, 1984)

———

Costly as it is, it would be difficult to describe the life of a successful young competitor as indulgent. They are, after all, skating six hours a day, six days a week, ten months out of the year. Many, if not most, are still putting in a full six-hour school day, which leaves about four hours for homework, family life, and growing up—with very little margin for laziness, rebellion, and weirding-out. Adults might not see a loss here, but we're speaking of the developmental rights of the young. Quite obviously, skaters this age cannot be expected to cover their own expenses. Moreover, regulations governing amateur competition prevent participants from earning a living at the thing they do best. Older skaters are obliged to find regular jobs (Jayne Torvill worked for an insurance company while her partner, Christopher Dean, delivered the mail) or find private sponsors, as did John Curry. Sonja Henie, clever girl, avoided all this. She was born wealthy and skated her way into another fortune later.

Whoever they are, whatever their means, they all head for the rink. They like to name rinks after people, it seems. There's the Dorothy Hamill in Connecticut, the Fritz Dietl in New Jersey, even a Von Braun in Huntsville, Alabama. There's a Grundy, a Snively, and a Benjamin Franklin Yack in the listings—as well as an Icelandia, Arctic Blades, Zero Temp and, calling it what it is, the Ice Box. Hundreds of these great refrigerated hangars dot the continent—by rough count, 89 in Massachusetts alone, 87 in New York, 55 in Michigan. That must be because people in cold climes are addictive about winter sports, right? Wrong. There are only 3 in Alaska, while there are 55 in California, a state that breeds a disproportionate number of champions (among them Tai Babilonia, Randy Gardner, Debi Thomas, Tiffany Chin, Brian Boitano). Of the hundreds of rinks with teaching programs, some 150 are affiliated with clubs endorsed by the United States Figure Skating Association (USFSA) which, in turn, is the only U.S. governing body recognized by the International Skating Union (ISU). The ISU regulates all international competition— the apogee of competitive skating.

Every celebrity skating biography bemoans the cold dark mornings at the rink—getting up at four in the morning to practice before school or work, returning afterward for still more practice and coaching. Peggy Fleming says she hated the cold before she ever dreamed of skating. Janet Lynn drove 150 miles daily just to get to the rink and back. Debi Thomas' mother did the same for her—meanwhile commuting to her own full-time job. Scholar-skaters Button, Albright, Petkevich, and Thomas have competed for academic honors as well, the first three at Harvard, the latter at Stanford; every spare minute spent cramming for

A firing squad of judges. They enforce rules few understand in an elaborate display of fairness qualifying subjective judgment—only to be judged themselves. (World F.S. Hall of Fame and Museum)

exams and papers, catching up on classwork missed during competitions. While this group might be described as non-stop achievers, they tend to look upon their academic careers as a healthy escape from competition, the principle of balance applied to private life. Asked if the twin demands of an academic and skating career weren't overwhelming, Microbiology major Debi Thomas replied, "I wasn't burdened with the pressure of knowing [skating] was all I had been working for."

The rink, hardly a pretty sight at five in the morning, compares in some respects to a full service department store for skaters—pro shops, snack shops, lockers, rental concessions, practice rooms, practice mini-rinks, coaching, contests, exhibitions, entertainments. One could easily visit one of these establishments without realizing it is *the* establishment, campus and college of organized skating. While some are better known than others—among them the Broadmoor in Colorado Springs and the Olympic Skating Complex in Lake Placid—there is, strictly speaking, no Juilliard School of Skating. If a rink is USFSA affiliated, it is constituent to a highly organized institution with a complex and demanding curriculum designed to preserve and perpetuate the best in skating. All internationally recognized skaters are, in a general sense, graduates of the same school, the same curriculum. The ISU insures that competitors the world over will follow the same syllabus, skate the same language, from first lesson to first place at the Olympics.

Herewith, in broad outline, the lesson plan. It is compiled and explained in the USFSA *Rulebook*—not something you'd skate with in one hand, mittens clutched in the other. Over 300 pages long, it compares for light reading with the boiler plate in your mortgage or lease. "The following Steps 20 to 27 skated in a Kilian hold, are interrupted by the lady skating a twizzle of one revolution on Step 22 under the man's left arm. . . . Steps 26–27 constitute a *chassé* and run respectively, followed by a A LFI turn. . . ." Essentially, the *Rulebook* answers the question "how do I become a champion?" the way Julia Child's two-volume classic answers the query, "what's for dinner?"

The short answer is that there are two basic disciplines in amateur figure skating—testing and competing—and the two are diabolically joined together. All three figure skating specialties—Singles, Pairs, and Dance—follow this same format with some variation. Limiting ourselves to Singles competition as a model, the generalization still holds that tests are intended to enforce a standard of excellence, while competing resolves whose best is best.

Before you can even take a test, you have to take a test—the so-called "prelims." These are a show of basic skating literacy. The skater is asked to skate the width of the rink in half circles of forward outside edges (skates naturally trace curves when you lean into an edge); a minimum of five must be completed on alternating feet. This is followed by the skating of three figures—a forward inside 8, a forward outside 8, and a waltz 8—each of which must be traced three times in succession, no stopping. The judge looks for steady clean curves, flexed knees, and proper pushes from the outside edge of the blade (never the toe).

Now all the skater has to do is pass eight tests, outskate the competition, and he can be champion of the world. There's a degree of truth in this myth, except in our narrative the skater-hero is literally tested at every turn: judges will get down on their hands and knees, on the ice, and try to fault the turns. The journey begins as the skater pushes off into the first figure of the first test. . . .

In all, there are eight figure skating tests and six freestyle tests a skater must pass to participate at the highest ranks of competition. These are administered one by one when, and as, the skater is ready for testing. The successful completion of each test entitles that skater to compete against skaters of equal accomplishment—juvenile against juvenile, senior against senior. Starting at the bottom and working through to the top, it would look like this:

USFSA TEST PASSED		COMPETITION LEVEL
2nd Figure and Juvenile Free Skating	=	Juvenile
3rd Figure and Intermediate Free Skating	=	Intermediate
4th or 5th Figure and Novice Free Skating	=	Novice
Junior Free Skating	=	Junior
Free Skating	=	Senior

The skater ascends both sides of the mountain, both the test hierarchy and the levels of competition. Beyond these rankings are the rankings of the competitions themselves. To begin with, there are non-qualifying and qualifying competitions. The latter is more prestigious, the former is considered good experience (competition for its own sake is not considered an embarrassment in the world of organized skating). Qualifying competitions are those sanctioned by the USFSA, the ones that move a skater forward, one by one, to the peak of a competitive career. As you might expect, these too are ranked: Regional, Sectional, and National.

QUALIFYING COMPETITIONS

REGIONALS

New England	Eastern Great Lakes	Central Pacific
North Atlantic	Southwestern	Northwest Pacific
South Atlantic	Upper Great Lakes	Southwest Pacific

SECTIONALS

Eastern	Midwestern	Pacific Coast

NATIONALS

WORLD CHAMPIONSHIPS
(Senior and Junior)

OLYMPIC WINTER GAMES

It is the confluence of the test program, the competition structure, and seeding of competitions themselves, that strikes sparks and makes reputations. The skater who has passed all the tests, competed as a senior, and won a national title, is the skater you start reading about in the newspapers. With few technical exceptions, the top three winners from the Nationals make up our World and Olympic teams.

Imagine the crisp sound of an Albinoni horn concerto ringing out over the ice and the still figure of a single skater dressed in white sweater and slacks. He seems to be improvising, skating to himself. He plays with edges, with forward and backward, with stop and go. Now see an arabesque glide through measure after measure of music, over yard upon yard of ice, until it winds down and freezes, in place, at music's end. This is John Curry skating a piece by Twyla Tharp—a modern idiomatic reflection on the principles and technique tested in every competitor's performance in both figure and free skating.

As with Czerny and the *pianoforte*, Ms. Tharp sees the beauty inherent in fundamentals. Unlike keyboard artists, however, skaters must run their scales and *arpeggios* in front of the judges: compulsory school figures count for 30 percent of the competitor's total score. Moreover, skaters don't know until just minutes before they perform which figures they'll be asked to skate. From a lexicon of 82 figures, several are selected in advance which the skaters are free to practice, but the final choice of three is left to the last moment. "In a deathly hush, the skater stands at the starting point of his figure. . . . For better or worse, he strikes off and the competition is on its way." Skater/instructor Robert Ogilvie narrates. "The figure is skated three times without pause . . . the judges start to walk all over the figure observing its good and bad points. . . . Examination of the turns usually involves a lot of bending down and kneeling on the ice. Judging has its own hazards and on rare occasions the sepulchral silence is broken by a judge falling over. . . ."

Most of us have never observed this event in progress because it isn't televised. Television executives have determined for us that we wouldn't find it interesting. Without debating their reliability in judging what is and isn't interesting, suffice it to say that many skaters—and enthusiasts—contest the importance of figures in competition. The argument runs that the skating of the modern age is freestyle and that figures are little more than a holdover from the past. Nearly a hundred years old, the schedule of 41 figures (counted as 82 when skated on each foot) was gleaned from a once expanding repertoire of literally hundreds of figure patterns, some of them extraordinarily complex. Great skaters prided themselves on the invention of new figures and wild moves. But there seemed to be no fair way to compare and judge such variety. Too, as interest in freestyle overtook the earlier fascination with figures, the focus shifted from the ice to the skater, and to the skater's form. The figure cutting a stunning figure did not always cut a stunning figure. So in 1892 the ISU settled upon a catechism of figures being skated to this day—effectively terminating further growth in this branch of skating.

While "figure" skating causes resentment and debate in some quarters, its defense is not unthinking nor merely conservative. Its advocacy, on the other hand, like the learning of multiplication tables, is not, perhaps, a dynamic way to seek public office. As designer of the USFSA Basic Test Program, Robert Ogilvie argues that figures importantly anchor the technique required for freestyle. "Any pro who has ever tried to teach freestyle to a powerful skater who has never done a figure in his life will tell you how very

difficult it is. Not only is all control over the edges lacking, but so is any understanding of the way in which his body works. If he is asked to pass the free leg forward and at the same time press the free hip back, he will look at the teacher as though he is out of his mind." Ogilvie lists what figures teach—and show—qualities judges will certainly discern in competition. Reviewing this list gives the nonparticipant a greater sense of what figures are about.

*Ability to hold an edge in various positions without losing control of the rotation.

*Ability to move various parts of the body in isolation, together, and in opposition.

*Ability to strike onto a true curve in the correct direction in relation to the preceding curve.

*Ability to execute all turns, fast and slow, with complete control.

*Development of equal ability on both sides of the body.

*Development of a physical point of reference.

*Sense of pattern round an axis.

*Stillness in the upper part of the body.

*Concentration.

*Discipline.

*Ability to execute well-shaped turns.

*Ability to execute all turns cleanly.

*Ability to trace in triple repetition.

(With permission, *Competitive Figure Skating*, Robert S. Ogilvie, Harper & Row, 1985)

Assuming, for the moment, all parties can agree that figures do promote excellence in freestyle, the question remains—must a skater pass all eight tests to learn what they have to teach? Further, if figures are seen as an adjunct to freestyle, what are they doing in the midst of competition? Why not a demonstration of jazz dance and weight lifting, also employed to improve freestyle?

The true answer is that figures are already fading as a serious consideration in competition, a fact clearly reflected in the scoring: once 50 percent of a skater's score, figures have given away twenty percentage points to freestyle scoring. We are caught, it seems, in transition. Anomalies of change are part of life and certainly a part of skating history. If it took the competitive establishment a hundred years to come in out of the cold, it's doubtful they will be rushed into a resolution of this other issue.

At last, we come to the freestyle portion of competition—free skating it is sometimes called—presented in two programs, one short, one long. The short program (20 percent of the total score) consists of required elements—jumps, spins, footwork—knit together by the contestant's choreography and selected music. Artistically, it is a little like fitting all the words from a vocabulary list into a single sentence. To call it free skating is stretching a point. The longer program (50 percent of the total score) is a different matter: at last the skater is given his freedom, within the restrictions of time: five minutes for men, four minutes for women. "In those minutes," coauthors Sheffield and Woodward write, are compressed "whatever can be said on skates about music and movement." "It is," they continue, "an interpretation of one of several pieces of music, a dramatization of one's character, a projection of skating style. A free skater can be neither all leaps and bounds nor a collection of adagio attitudes. Judges grade both the artistic intent and actual execution. . . . They consider degree of daring; elements of surprise or elegance; changes of tempo; breadth of interpretive ambition; use of ice area; the number, height, and spacing of the jumps. . . ."

It's the jumps that unlock the danger implicit in skating. Most readers would recognize their names—recognizing them in performance is something else again. There are 47 jumps and jump variants listed in the USFSA *Rulebook*—each identified by edge, position of body before lift-off, and use (or not) of the free foot (toe) for leverage. Double Salchow, Delayed Axel, Toe Walley, Half Lutz—all fractions and multiples of classic jumps—are just words to many of us, words that signal something big is about to happen. To give you some idea of their difficulty, here is what those four jumps—in basic form—look like on paper:

THE AXEL: A jump launched from a forward outside edge, of one-and-a-half revolutions, landed on a back outside edge.

Debi Thomas. (Margaret S. Williamson)

Among the group: Linda Fratianne, Tai Babilonia, Randy Gardner, Jojo Starbuck, Ken Shelley. (Margaret S. Williamson)

THE LUTZ: A toe-assisted jump, of one revolution, launched and landed by a back outside edge.

THE WALLEY: A one revolution jump launched by a back inside edge, landed by a back outside edge—same foot—winding counter to the natural spinning direction of the launching edge.

THE SALCHOW: A one revolution jump launched by a back inside edge, landed by a back outside edge.

If in his jumps the skater seems to defy and triumph over the ice, in the spinning he tempts and exploits it, shows it off to full advantage. Noting the accelerated rotation achieved by pulling the arms in tight to the body, Harvard scientist Owen Gingerich observed that this is the conservation of angular momentum at work: "The same sort of thing happens in stars as they collapse." A technique that can be used as a kind of elegant unwinding or unfolding—or as dramatically as a drum-roll—it nearly defies lucid technical description. "To my eye he was a blurred scarlet pillar," Professor Gingerich said of the skater's Scratch Spin he'd photographed, "but the $\frac{1}{125}$-shutter speed froze his rotation. . . . The only way my class will know he was really spinning is from his hair, whirling straight out like a quattrocento halo." Technically speaking, the skater had entered the spin on a deep forward outside edge forming a tight spiraling curve, the free leg was brought in flexed high and akimbo until the spinning point was reached, at which time the hands and feet were drawn into the body and pressed downward to achieve maximum speed.

Crossfoot, Camel, Broken Leg, Sit Spin, these together with the jumps and a variety of miscellaneous moves like Spirals, Spreadeagles, and Butterflys, make for the moments people remember. Once in a great while they make history.

The athleticism of Dick Button's skating together with the jumps he pioneered are seen and remembered now in the skating of all young competitors. Since the time of their introduction, triple jumps have become a staple item in all competitive freestyle programs; indeed, they blithely are tossed off by young hot-shots in arenas all over the country—to the dismay of some coaches like Olympic medalist Cecilia Colledge. "See that," she says, watching a twelve-year-old fall out of yet another triple jump, "they don't even *try* to save it."

Ms. Colledge is speaking of the dignity, finesse, she believes make for great skating. Many would agree. In an interview from the Calgary Olympics, champion Barbara Ann Scott referred peevishly to "those cursed triple jumps." Certainly jump-lust increasingly pulls freestyle programs way out of shape.

Meanwhile, quadruple jumps, already solved in practice, soon will be successfully introduced in competition. The grim prospect of the freestyle program becoming, more than ever, a tense display of tricks and poses set in a mindless aspic of pop music looms before us.

But skating history has a way of righting itself. Perhaps ice dancing will lead the way. For it is the "dancers" with their disciplined deep edges, musicality, and stipulated absence of daredevil tricks—that are now attracting world attention to the sport. Straight 6.0's for Torvill and Dean's dramatic interpretations at the 1984 Olympics perfectly reflected popular sentiment: this was something special. Not surprisingly, the audience for the skating segments of the 1988 telecasts were huge. Yet the dancers pulled back, reverting to the commonplaces of the ballroom. Only one couple, the Duschesneys of Canada, showed us something fresh—escaping in a tangle of limbs across the ice, like fugitives, to the pulsing sound of jungle drums. The piece, we learned, was choreographed by Christopher Dean, Jayne Torvill's partner. It received a quarreling spread of scores ranging from 5.0 to 5.7—which is roughly equivalent to saying it was awful, it was wonderful. Both were right. And the performance got there the best possible way—taking risks and owing everything to a vision of what skating could be. "Show me," John Curry instructs his youngest pupils, "something you think is beautiful."

It seems a good place to begin and end.

GLOSSARY OF SKATING TERMS

ARABIAN: flying spin launched by both feet; body, legs, and arms are stretched parallel to the ice.

AXEL: jump of one-and-a-half revolutions launched by a forward outside edge and landed by a back outside edge on the other foot.

BIELMAN SPIN: one-foot spin in which the free leg is lifted, grasped, and fully extended behind the arched body of the skater.

BRACKET: figure-skating turn of direction leading away from the circle in the figure being traced, executed by a change of edge.

CAMEL: spin in arabesque position.

CHOCTAW: change from forward to backward motion involving a change of both foot and edge.

COMPULSORY DANCE: an established set-pattern dance with specific steps, timing, rhythm, partner positions, and musical mood; the first of three events in ice dancing competition.

CRANSTON CAMEL: back camel in which the free leg is bent and pressed back at the knee with one hand opening the hip position wide.

CROSSFOOT SPIN: two-foot spin on outside edges in which one foot is crossed over the other.

CROSSOVERS: in stroking, the leading foot crosses in front of the other foot and sets down on the blade's inside edge while the other foot trails on an outside edge.

DEATHDROP: Arabian launched on one foot and ending in a back-sit spin.

DEATH SPIRAL: a pair move in which the man swings the woman around him as he pivots in position; the woman's body appears fully extended, head grazing the ice.

EDGES: the two sharpened sides of the hollow running the length of the skate blade. The skater "takes an edge" by leaning as he moves. Edges are designated forward, backward, inside, and outside, and are employed almost at all times.

FIGURES: the eight and variations thereof (along with the three) comprise compulsory school figures.

FLIP: toe-assisted one-revolution jump.

FOOTWORK: succession of steps, turns, hops, and positions.

FREE SKATING: a more technical term for freestyle.

FREESTYLE: jumps, spins, and footwork performed to music in singles skating.

ICE DANCING: a discipline combining both compulsory "set-pattern" dance presentation and a free dance of the skaters' own invention. "Freedom" is limited by restrictions on lifting, spinning and time/distance limitations on separation of the partners.

LONG PROGRAM: the freestyle program in the singles event accounting for 50 percent of the total mark in competition and 71 percent of the total mark in the pairs event.

LOOP JUMP: one-revolution edge jump launched from a back outside edge and landed on the back outside edge of the same foot.

ORIGINAL SET-PATTERN DANCE: A set-pattern dance with prescribed rhythm created by the couple performing.

PATCH: that piece of ice rented by the skater for practicing figures. Regulation rinks must minimally measure 185 by 85 feet and generally divide into 20 patches.

RADIUS: seen in profile, the curve of the blade from toe to heel.

ROCKER: oversimplified, a turn from forward to backward.

ROLL: a deep outside edge.

RUSSIAN SPLIT: toe-touching split jump.

SALCHOW: edge jump launched from a back inside edge, moving through one revolution in the air, and landed by the back outside edge of the opposite foot.

SCRIBE: a large compass used to draw geometric circles on the ice as patterns for the aspiring figure skater.

SERPENTINE: three-circle figure or reference to footwork winding back and forth across the ice.

SHORT PROGRAM: freestyle presentation in both singles and pairs events made up of required elements accounting for 20 percent of singles total score in competition, and 29 percent of the pairs score.

SPIRAL: a sustained gliding arabesque—mysteriously named.

SPREADEAGLE: two-foot glide in fifth position.

STAG: split jump in which the leading leg is bent.

TOE PICKS: teeth on the front of the skate blade.

WALLEY: one-revolution jump launched off a back inside edge and landed by back outside edge—same foot.

ZAMBONI: the machine that cuts the rutted ice, lays down fresh water, and creates a clean new surface.

BIBLIOGRAPHY

Aspin, Jehosophat. *A Picture of the Manners, Customs, Sports, and Pastimes of England. . . .* London: J. Harris, 1825.

Bass, Howard. *The International Encyclopedia of Winter Sports.* Cranbury, N.J.: Great Albion Books, 1971.

Bass, Howard. *Winter Sports.* New York: A.S. Barnes and Company, 1966.

Bell, William Perkins. *From Rattlesnake Hunt to Hockey.* Canada: 1934.

Boulton, William. *Amusements of Old London.* London: John C. Nimmo, 1901.

Brokaw, Irving. *The Art of Skating.* New York: Charles Scribner's Sons, 1926.

Browne, George Henry. *A Handbook of Figure Skating.* Springfield, Mass.: Barney and Berry, 1913.

Browne, George Henry. *The New Skating.* Cambridge, Mass.: 1910.

Button, Dick. *Dick Button on Skates.* London: Peter Davies, 1956.

Clark, Kenneth. *Civilisation.* New York: Harper & Row, 1969.

Curry, Manfred. *The Beauty of Skating.* New York: Charles Scribner's Sons, 1936.

Dulles, Foster Rhea. *America Learns to Play.* New York: D. Appleton Century Company, 1940.

Foster, Fredrick W. *A Bibliography of Skating.* London: B.W. Warhurst, 1898.

Fowler, George Herbert. *On the Outside Edge.* London: H. Cox, 1897.

Gill, Edward. *The Skater's Manual.* New York: Andrew Peck and Company, 1867.

Goodfellow, Arthur. *Wonderful World of Skates.* Mountainburg, Ark.: 1972.

Goodman, Neville. *Handbook of Fen Skating.* London: Sampson, Low, Marston, Searle, and Rivington, 1882.

Grayden, Alex. *Memoirs of a Life, Chiefly Passed in Philadelphia.* Harrisburg, Pa.: 1811.

Heathecote, John Moyer, and Tebbutt, C.G. *Skating.* London: Longmans, Green and Company, 1892.

Heller, Mark, ed. *Illustrated Encyclopedia of Skating.* New York: Paddington Press, 1979.

Henie, Sonja. *Wings on My Feet.* Englewood Cliffs, N.J.: Prentice-Hall, 1940.

Hennessy, John. *Torvill and Dean.* London: David and Charles, 1984.

Hibbert, Christopher. *London.* New York: Penguin Books, 1980.

Kent, Col. H.V. *Dancing on Skates.* London: R.E. Ward and Sons, 1910.

Kouwenhoven, John A. *The Columbia Historical Portrait of New York.* New York: Harper & Row, 1972.

Lambert, Luna. *The American Skating Mania.* Washington, D.C.: Smithsonian Institution Press, 1979.

Latham, Robert. *The Illustrated Pepys.* Los Angeles: University of California Press, 1978.

Law, Ernest. *Valsing on Ice.* London: H. Rees, 1910.

Levetus, A.S. *Imperial Vienna.* London: The Bodley Head.

Lewis, John Fredrick. *Skating and the Philadelphia Skating Club.* Philadelphia: 1895.

Manchester, Herbert. *Four Centuries of Sport in America.* Derrydale Press, 1931.

Meagher, George A. *Figure and Fancy Skating.* London: Bliss, Sands, and Foster, 1895.

Meyer, Bror. *Skating with Bror Meyer.* Garden City, N.Y.: Doubleday, Page and Martin, 1921.

Money, Keith. *John Curry.* New York: Alfred A. Knopf, 1978.

Monier-Williams, Montagu Sneade. *Figure Skating.* The Isthmian Library. London: A.D. Innes and Company, 1898.

Oelschlagel, Charlotte. *Hippodrome Skating Book.* New York: Hippodrome Skating Club, 1916.

Ogilvie, Robert S. *Competitive Figure Skating.* New York: Harper & Row, 1985.

Pachter, Marc, and Wein, Frances Stevenson, eds. *Abroad in America.* Reading, Mass.: Addison-Wesley Publishing Company, 1976.

Patterson, Jerry E. *The City of New York.* New York: Harry N. Abrams, 1978.

Peek, Hedley. *The Poetry of Sport.* London: Longmans, Green and Company, 1896.

Petkevich, John Misha. *The Skater's Handbook.* New York: Charles Scribner's Sons, 1984.

Putnam, Harold, and Parkinson, Dwight. *Skating.* New York: A.S. Barnes and Company, 1939.

Reeves, Boleyne, ed. *Sports and Pastimes in Town and Country.* London: T.H. Coe, 1841.

Robinson, Fletcher, ed. *Ice Sports.* The Isthmian Library. London: Ward, Lock and Company, 1901.

Sheffield, Robert, and Woodward, Richard. *The Ice Skating Book.* New York: Universe Books, 1980.

Stephenson, Lois and Richard. *A History and Annotated Bibliography of Skating Costume.* Meriden, Conn.: Bayberry Hill Press, 1970.

Styer, Robert A. *The Encyclopedia of Hockey.* New York: A.S. Barnes and Company, 1970.

Swift, Frank. *The Skater's Textbook.* New York: Gray and Green, Printers, 1868.

Syers, Edgar and Madge. *The Book of Winter Sports.* London: E. Arnold, 1908.

Tocqueville, Alexis de. *Democracy in America.* New York: Oxford University Press, 1947.

Trease, Geoffrey. *Samuel Pepys and his World.* New York: G.P. Putnam Sons, 1972.

Tunis, John R. *Democracy and Sport.* New York: A.S. Barnes and Company, 1941.

Twombly, Wells. *200 Years of American Sport.* New York: McGraw-Hill Book Company, 1976.

Vinson, Maribel Yerxa. *Advanced Figure Skating.* New York: McGraw-Hill Book Company, 1940.

Vinson, Maribel Yerxa. *Primer of Figure Skating.* New York: McGraw-Hill Book Company, 1938.

Walker, John George. *A Handbook of Swimming and Skating.* London: G. Routledge and Company, 1858.

Walker, Robert. *Amusements and Sports in American Life.* Chicago: University of Chicago Press, 1939.

Wright, Benjamin T. *Reader's Guide to Figure Skating's Hall of Fame.* Boston: United States Figure Skating Association, 1978.

OLYMPIC SKATING RECORDS
(Figure Skating)

Men

	GOLD	SILVER	BRONZE
1908 London	Ulrich Salchow (Sweden)	Richard Johansson (Sweden)	Per Thorén (Sweden)
1920 Antwerp	Gillis Grafström (Sweden)	Andreas Krogh (Norway)	Martin Stixrud (Norway)
1924 Chamonix	Gillis Grafström (Sweden)	Willy Böckl (Austria)	Georg Gautschi (Switzerland)
1928 St. Moritz	Gillis Grafström (Sweden)	Willy Böckl (Austria)	Bobby van Zeebroeck (Belgium)
1932 Lake Placid	Karl Schäfer (Austria)	Gillis Grafström (Sweden)	Montgomery Wilson (Canada)
1936 Garmisch	Karl Schäfer (Austria)	Ernst Baier (Germany)	Felix Kasper (Austria)
1948 St. Moritz	Dick Button (USA)	Hans Gerschwiler (Switzerland)	Edi Rada (Austria)
1952 Oslo	Dick Button (USA)	Helmut Seibt (Austria)	James Grogan (USA)
1956 Cortina	Hayes Jenkins (USA)	Ronald Robertson (USA)	David Jenkins (USA)
1960 Squaw Valley	David Jenkins (USA)	Carol Divin (Czechoslovakia)	Donald Jackson (Canada)
1964 Innsbruck	Manfred Schnelldorfer (Germany)	Alain Calmat (France)	Scott Allen (USA)
1968 Grenoble	Wolfgang Schwarz (Austria)	Tim Wood (USA)	Patrick Pera (France)
1972 Sapporo	Ondrej Nepela (Czechoslovakia)	Sergei Chetverukhin (USSR)	Patrick Pera (France)
1976 Innsbruck	John Curry (Great Britain)	Vladimir Kovalev (USSR)	Toller Cranston (Canada)
1980 Lake Placid	Robin Cousins (Great Britain)	Jan Hoffman (East Germany)	Charles Tickner (USA)
1984 Sarajevo	Scott Hamilton (USA)	Brian Orser (Canada)	Joseph Jozefsobovick (Czechoslovakia)
1988 Calgary	Brian Boitano (USA)	Brian Orser (Canada)	Viktor Petrenko (USSR)

Women

	GOLD	SILVER	BRONZE
1908 London	Madge Syers (Great Britain)	Elsa Rendschmidt (Germany)	Dorothy Grennhough- Smith (Great Britain)
1920 Antwerp	Magda Julin-Mauroy (Sweden)	Svea Norén (Sweden)	Theresa Weld (USA)

	GOLD	SILVER	BRONZE
1924 Chamonix	Herma Plank-Szabo (Austria)	Beatrix Loughran (USA)	Ethel Muckelt (Great Britain)
1928 St. Moritz	Sonja Henie (Norway)	Fritzi Burger (Austria)	Beatrix Loughran (USA)
1932 Lake Placid	Sonja Henie (Norway)	Fritzi Burger (Austria)	Maribel Vinson (USA)
1936 Garmisch	Sonja Henie (Norway)	Cecilia Colledge (Great Britain)	Vivi-Anne Hultén (Sweden)
1948 St. Moritz	Barbara Ann Scott (Canada)	Eva Pawlik (Austria)	Jeannette Altwegg (Great Britain)
1952 Oslo	Jeannette Altwegg (Great Britain)	Tenley Albright (USA)	Jacqueline du Bief (France)
1956 Cortina	Tenley Albright (USA)	Carol Heiss (USA)	Ingrid Wendl (Austria)
1960 Squaw Valley	Carol Heiss (USA)	Sjoukje Dijkstra (Netherlands)	Barbara Roles (USA)
1964 Innsbruck	Sjoukje Dijkstra (Netherlands)	Regine Heitzer (Austria)	Petra Burka (Canada)
1968 Grenoble	Peggy Fleming (USA)	Gabriele Seyfert (East Germany)	Hana Maskova (Czechoslovakia)
1972 Sapporo	Beatrix Schuba (Austria)	Karen Magnussen (Canada)	Janet Lynn (USA)
1976 Innsbruck	Dorothy Hamill (USA)	Dianne de Leeuw (Netherlands)	Christine Errath (East Germany)
1980 Lake Placid	Anett Pötzsch (East Germany)	Linda Fratianne (USA)	Dagmar Lurz (West Germany)
1984 Sarajevo	Katarina Witt (East Germany)	Rosalynn Sumners (USA)	Kira Ivanova (USSR)
1988 Calgary	Katarina Witt (East Germany)	Elizabeth Manley (Canada)	Debi Thomas (USA)

Pairs

	GOLD	SILVER	BRONZE
1908 London	Heinrich Burger Anna Hübler (Germany)	James Johnson Phyllis Johnson (Great Britain)	Edgar Syers Madge Syers (Great Britain)
1920 Antwerp	Walter Jakobsson Ludowika Eilers (Finland)	Yngvar Bryn Alexia Schöyen (Norway)	Basil Williams Phyllis Johnson (Great Britain)
1924 Chamonix	Alfred Berger Helene Engelmann (Austria)	Walter Jakobsson Ludowika Eilers (Finland)	Pierre Brunet Andrée Joly (France)
1928 St. Moritz	Pierre Brunet Andrée Joly (France)	Otto Kaiser Lilly Scholz (Austria)	Ludwig Wrede Melitta Brunner (Austria)
1932 Lake Placid	Pierre Brunet Andrée Joly (France)	Sherwin Badger Beatrix Loughran (USA)	Läszlo Szollás Emilie Rotter (Hungary)

	GOLD	SILVER	BRONZE
1936 Garmisch	Ernst Baier Maxie Herber (Germany)	Erich Pausin Ilse Pausin (Austria)	László Szollás Emilie Rotter (Hungary)
1948 St. Moritz	Pierre Baugniet Micheline Lannoy (Belgium)	Ede Király Andrea Kékesy (Hungary)	Wallace Distelmeyer Suzanne Morrow (Canada)
1952 Oslo	Paul Falk Ria Baran (Germany)	Peter Kennedy Karol Kennedy (USA)	Laszlo Nagy Marianne Nagy (Hungary)
1956 Cortina	Kurt Oppelt Sissy Schwarz (Austria)	Norris Bowden Frances Dafoe (Canada)	Laszlo Nagy Marianne Nagy (Hungary)
1960 Squaw Valley	Robert Paul Barbara Wagner (Canada)	Hans-Jürgen Bäumler Marika Kilius (Germany)	Ronald Ludington Nancy Ludington (USA)
1964 Innsbruck	Oleg Protopopov Ludmila Belousova (USSR)	Hans-Jürgen Bäumler Marika Kilius (Germany)	Guy Revell Debbi Wilkes (Canada)
1968 Grenoble	Oleg Protopopov Ludmila Belousova (USSR)	Aleksandr Gorelik Tatjana Zhuk (USSR)	Wolfgang Danne Margot Glockshuber (West Germany)
1972 Sapporo	Alexsei Ulanov Irina Rodnina (USSR)	Andrei Suraikin Ludmila Smirnova (USSR)	Uwe Kagelmann Manuela Gross (East Germany)
1976 Innsbruck	Aleksandr Zaitsev Irina Rodnina (USSR)	Rolf Oesterreich Romy Kermer (East Germany)	Uwe Kagelmann Manuela Gross (East Germany)
1980 Lake Placid	Aleksandr Zaitsev Irina Rodnina (USSR)	Sergei Shakrai Marina Cherkasova (USSR)	Uwe Bewersdorff Manuela Mager (East Germany)
1984 Sarajevo	Oleg Vasiliev Elena Valova (USSR)	Peter Carruthers Kitty Carruthers (USA)	Selezneva Makarov (USSR)
1988 Calgary	Sergei Grinkov Yekaterina Gordeyeva (USSR)	Oleg Vasiliev Elena Valova (USSR)	Peter Oppegard Jill Watson (USA)

Ice Dance

	GOLD	SILVER	BRONZE
1976 Innsbruck	Aleksandr Gorshkov Ludmila Pakhomova (USSR)	Andrei Minenkov Irina Moiseeva (USSR)	Jim Millns Colleen O'Connor (USA)
1980 Lake Placid	Gennadi Karponosov Natalia Linichuk (USSR)	Andras Sallay Krisztina Regoczy (Hungary)	Andrei Minenkov Irina Moiseeva (USSR)
1984 Sarajevo	Christopher Dean Jayne Torvill (Great Britain)	Andrei Bukin Natalya Bestemianova (USSR)	Sergei Ponomarenko Marina Klimova (USSR)
1988 Calgary	Andrei Bukin Natalya Bestemianova (USSR)	Sergei Ponomarenko Marina Klimova (USSR)	Robert McCall Tracy Wilson (Canada)

Portfolio of Stars

Peggy Fleming

Debi Thomas

Katarina Witt

Elaine Zayak

Elizabeth Manley

Linda Fratianne

Rosalynn Sumners

Caryn Kadavy   Kira Ivanova

Tiffany Chin   Jill Trenary

Janet Lynn

Dorothy Hamill

Midori Ito

Anett Poetzsch

Brian Boitano

Brian Orser

John Curry

Scott Hamilton

Robin Cousins

Christopher Bowman

Yekaterina Gordeyeva and Sergei Grinkov

Ludmila and Oleg Protopopov

Gillian Wachsman and Todd Waggoner

Jill Watson and Peter Oppegard

Kitty and Peter Carruthers

Jojo Starbuck and Ken Shelley

Tai Babilonia and Randy Gardner

Elena Valova and Oleg Vasiliev

Irina Rodnina and Aleksander Zaitzev

Tracy Wilson and Robert McCall

Jayne Torvill and Christopher Dean

PEGGY FLEMING (USA). Olympic gold medalist, 1968; World Champion, 1966–68. (Photo: Christie Jenkins)

DEBI THOMAS (USA). Olympic bronze medalist, 1988; World Champion, 1986. (Photo: Christie Jenkins)

KATARINA WITT (East Germany). Olympic gold medalist, 1988, 1984; World Champion, 1987, 1984–85. (Photo: Howey Caufman)

ELAINE ZAYAK (USA). World Champion 1982; National Ladies Champion, 1981. (Photo: Michael A. Esposito, Jr.)

ELIZABETH MANLEY (Canada). Olympic silver medalist, 1988. Canadian Ladies Champion, 1987. (Photo: Michael A. Esposito, Jr.)

LINDA FRATIANNE (USA). Olympic silver medalist, 1980; World Champion 1979, 1977. (Photo: Christie Jenkins)

ROSALYNN SUMNERS (USA). Olympic silver medalist, 1984; World Champion, 1983. (Photo: Christie Jenkins)

CARYN KADAVY (USA). Olympic skating team, 1988; World bronze medalist, 1987. (Photo: Michael A. Esposito, Jr.)

KIRA IVANOVA (USSR). Olympic bronze medalist, 1984. (Photo: © Dave Black/Focus West)

TIFFANY CHIN (USA). World bronze medalist 1985–86; National Ladies Champion, 1985. (Photo: Howey Caufman)

JILL TRENARY (USA). Olympic skating team, 1988; National Ladies Champion, 1987. (Photo: © Focus West)

JANET LYNN (USA). Olympic bronze medalist, 1972; National Ladies Champion 1969–73. (Photo: Christie Jenkins)

DOROTHY HAMILL (USA). Olympic gold medalist, 1976; World Champion, 1976. (Photo: Christie Jenkins)

MIDORI ITO (Japan). Olympic skating team, 1988. (Photo: Manny Millan/Sports Illustrated)

ANETT POETZSCH (East Germany). Olympic gold medalist, 1980; World Champion, 1980, 1978. (Photo: Manny Millan/Sports Illustrated)

BRIAN BOITANO (USA). Olympic gold medalist, 1988; World Champion, 1986. (Photo: Christie Jenkins)

BRIAN ORSER (Canada). Olympic silver medalist, 1988; World Champion, 1987; Olympic silver medalist, 1984. (Photo: © Dave Black/Focus West)

TOLLER CRANSTON (Canada). Olympic bronze medalist, 1976; Canadian Men's Champion, 1971–76. (Photo: Howey Caufman)

JOHN CURRY (Great Britain). Olympic gold medalist, 1976; World Champion, 1976. (Photo: Christie Jenkins)

SCOTT HAMILTON (USA). Olympic gold medalist, 1984; World Champion, 1981–84. (Photo: Christie Jenkins)

ROBIN COUSINS (Great Britain). Olympic gold medalist, 1980. (Photo: Christie Jenkins)

CHRISTOPHER BOWMAN (USA). Olympic skating team, 1988; National Men's second. (Photo: Christie Jenkins)

YEKATERINA GORDEYEVA and SERGEI GRINKOV (USSR). Olympic gold medalists, pairs, 1988; World Champions, 1986–87. (Photo: © Dave Black/Focus West)

LUDMILA and OLEG PROTOPOPOV (USSR). Olympic gold medalists, pairs, 1968, 1964. World Champions, 1965–68. (Photo: Christie Jenkins)

GILLIAN WACHSMAN and TODD WAGGONER (USA). National Pair Champions, 1986. (Photo: Howey Caufman)

JILL WATSON and PETER OPPEGARD (USA). Olympic bronze medalists, pairs, 1988; National Pair Champions, 1987. (Photo: Howey Caufman)

KITTY and PETER CARRUTHERS (USA). Olympic silver medalists, pairs, 1984; National Pair Champions, 1981–84. (Photo: Michael A. Esposito, Jr.)

JOJO STARBUCK and KEN SHELLEY (USA). National Pairs Champions, 1970–72; World bronze medalists, pairs, 1971. (Photo: Christie Jenkins)

TAI BABILONIA and RANDY GARDNER (USA). World Pairs Champions, 1979; National Pairs Champions, 1976–80.(Photo: Christie Jenkins)

ELENA VALOVA and OLEG VASILIEV (USSR). Olympic silver medalists, pairs, 1988; Olympic gold medalists, pairs, 1984. (Photo: Christie Jenkins)

IRINA RODNINA and ALEKSANDER ZAITZEV (USSR). Olympic gold medalists, pairs, 1980, 1976. (Photo: Heinz Kluetmeier/Sports Illustrated)

TRACY WILSON and ROBERT MCCALL (Canada). Olympic bronze medalists, dance, 1988; World bronze medalists, 1987; Canadian Dance Champions, 1982–87. (Photo: Michael A Esposito, Jr.)

JAYNE TORVILL and CHRISTOPHER DEAN (Great Britain). Olympic gold medalists, 1984; British Dance Champions, 1979–84. (Photo: Christie Jenkins)